Praise for Anna Deavere Smith's

NOTES FROM THE FIELD

"Devastating. . . . Astonishing. . . . Unquestionably great theater."
—*Vulture*

"Brilliant. . . . Anna Deavere Smith may be the most empathetic person in America."
—*HuffPost*

"[A] masterpiece. . . . Smith's powerful style of living journalism uses the collective, cathartic nature of the theater to move us from despair toward hope."
—*The Village Voice*

"Urgently timely. . . . Audacious and mind-opening."
—*Time Out New York*

"This is captivating political theatre, a devastating document of racial inequality and the most rousing of rallying calls. Everyone should watch it."
—*The Guardian*

"A tour de force. . . . A coruscating indictment of the school-to-prison pipeline."
—*Financial Times*

"Stirring. . . . Powerful. . . . The scope is almost Shakespearean: the voices range from policy professionals to people on the street. If there's an overarching thrust . . . it lies in the suggestion that the struggle for civil rights is ongoing: the legacy of segregation, its trauma too, endures and reasserts itself."

—*The Telegraph* (London)

Anna Deavere Smith

NOTES FROM THE FIELD

Anna Deavere Smith is an actress, teacher, and playwright and the creator of the acclaimed *On the Road* series of one-woman plays, which are based on her interviews with diverse voices from communities in crisis. A recipient of the National Humanities Medal from President Obama and two Obie Awards, her work has also been nominated for a Pulitzer and two Tonys. Onscreen, she has appeared in many films and television shows, including *Philadelphia*, *The West Wing*, *Black-ish*, and *Nurse Jackie*. She is University Professor in the department of Art & Public Policy at NYU, where she also directs the Institute on the Arts and Civic Dialogue.

ALSO BY ANNA DEAVERE SMITH

Letters to a Young Artist

House Arrest and Piano

Talk to Me

Twilight: Los Angeles, 1992

Fires in the Mirror

NOTES FROM THE FIELD

NOTES FROM THE FIELD

ANNA DEAVERE SMITH

ANCHOR BOOKS

A Division of Penguin Random House LLC

New York

AN ANCHOR BOOKS ORIGINAL, MAY 2019

The Library of Congress Cataloging-in-Publication Data
Name: Smith, Anna Deavere, author.
Title: Notes from the field / by Anna Deavere Smith.
Description: New York : Anchor Books, a division of Penguin Random
House LLC, 2019. | "An Anchor Books original."
Identifiers: LCCN 2018040656 (print) | LCCN 2018051227 (ebook)
Subjects: LCSH: Minority students—United States—Drama. | Monologues, American. |
United States—Race relations—Drama.
Classification: LCC PS3569.M465 N68 2019 | DDC 812/.54—dc23
LC record available at https://lccn.loc.gov/2018040656

Anchor Books Trade Paperback ISBN: 978-0-525-56459-1
eBook ISBN: 978-0-525-56460-7

Book design by Anna B. Knighton

www.anchorbooks.com

Printed in the United States of America
10   9   8   7   6   5   4   3   2   1

In Memory of

Anna Young Smith,

Dr. Maxine Greene,

and Mr. Jonathan Demme

CONTENTS

INTRODUCTION

Notes from the Field is the most recent installment in what I consider my life's work: a series of plays I call *On the Road: A Search for American Character*. Since the 1980s, I have periodically traveled around America, interviewing large numbers of people, collecting their words and performing them onstage, crafting them into multivoiced solo dramas that bear witness to particular historical moments. I've created about twenty of these pieces over the past four decades, including *Fires in the Mirror* (in response to the 1991 riots in Crown Heights, Brooklyn) and *Twilight: Los Angeles, 1992* (about the riots). *Notes from the Field*, my latest effort, concerns what has come to be known among social scientists, educators, jurists, politicians, and activists as "the school-to-prison pipeline."

I view my plays as documentations of moments in history. Central to my creative process is active listening. My goal is to pay careful attention to the people I interview and then to reflect back what I have heard in the hope of sparking a conversation, of making change possible. I aim not to merely imitate but to study people closely enough so that I can embody them on the stage, using my own voice and body. When I was a girl, my grandfather told me, "If you say a word often enough, it becomes you." People speak of putting themselves into other people's shoes. My way of doing that is to put myself into other people's words.

It all starts with listening.

My process in creating *Notes from the Field* was the same one that I have used across my career. I interviewed about 250 people for this play, in four different geographic regions: Maryland, South Carolina, Northern California, and Pennsylvania. From out of the wealth of interview material that I amassed using the rehearsal processes for five different productions and some staged readings, I chose nineteen people to perform. The voices I selected reflect the variety of people caught up in the school-to-prison pipeline: students, parents, counselors, administrators, prisoners, preachers, politicians. Among them are Sherrilyn Ifill, president of the NAACP Legal Defense and Educational Fund; Reverend Jamal Harrison Bryant, who spoke at the funeral of Freddie Gray; Bree Newsome, a young activist arrested for removing the Confederate flag from the South Carolina State House; and Niya Kenny, a high school student who was arrested for protesting the violent treatment of a classmate by a school police officer. I end the play with Congressman John Lewis because he personifies both a violent moment in American history—the civil rights movement—and the promise of what American character is all about.

While the script of *Notes from the Field* was still a work in progress, I performed it in workshops around the country. I tried out different versions in different places, engaging local communities in a series of exchanges that helped to shape the piece.

The project really started as a social justice project. Each night in Berkeley, California, at Berkeley Repertory Theatre, and subsequently at the American Repertory Theater housed at Harvard University in Cambridge, Massachusetts, I literally stopped the show in the middle and told the audience they were "the second act" of the play. It was an enormous undertaking. We trained facilitators and divided audiences of five hundred people into groups of twenty. We then sent them around the theater, into spaces that they would normally not inhabit—paint shops and the artistic director's office—and spaces they do inhabit, like lobbies, front lawns, and bar-restaurant areas. I was trying to use the convening power of the theater to get strangers talking to one another about education, about race relations, about inequality, about violence, about what they as individuals could do. We asked people to say how proximate they were to the problem.

Nonprofit and for-profit US theater audiences are composed, for the most part, of middle-aged and middle- and upper-middle-class individuals—subscribers. At the same time, we were able to gather audiences of people from various communities at the American Repertory Theater, thanks in part to the support of Harvard's then president Drew Faust. One night the athletic teams came. Attendance was required for all freshmen.

Every night we performed at Berkeley and at the American Repertory Theater, we chose a person from the community—a restauranteur, a police officer, a student, an ex-offender, a religious leader—to welcome the audience and to say why they had come. This, to me, exemplifies what artistic institutions can be in their communities—places where a radical welcome is extended, where a radical hospitality is offered. We need spaces to bring us out into civic space, beyond our comfort zones, out from behind our metaphoric gates and picket fences, away for a moment from the TV, laptop, and smartphone screens that project back to us what we choose to see and hear.

My goal in all of this? To inspire action. To suggest to the youngest person in the crowd that they have agency. And we recently saw evidence of this. We saw in the US a movement among high school students sparked by the shooting at Stoneman Douglas High School in Parkland, Florida. One scholar of American education, Pedro Noguera, whom I at one time portrayed in *Notes from the Field*, predicted when I interviewed him in 2015 that activism would be more likely to happen in high school than in colleges due to the cost of attaining a college education and the pressures on college students.

In its final theatrical form, *Notes from the Field* was staged off-Broadway in New York City in 2016. It was subsequently adapted into a feature film by HBO that released in 2018. The text of this book combines the scripts of two of the stage productions while also bringing in elements from the HBO film.

It is my hope that the film can reach a wider audience—including young people, teachers, police officers, and others who don't typically go to the theater—and that it can usefully contribute to an ongoing debate. Since I first began working on this project, the issues have taken on an even greater urgency.

I vividly remember the exact moment that led me to this subject. It was an incident that occurred while I was filming the television series *Nurse Jackie*. I was in hair and makeup next to a castmate, British actress Eve Best, and I told her I couldn't get out of my mind a news story I had just heard: that a kid in Baltimore, my hometown, had peed in a water cooler at school and they were going to send him to jail. Eve responded, in her fabulous accent, "Oh, well, whatever happened to mischief?"

That was when it struck me: rich kids get mischief, poor kids get pathologized and incarcerated. Data released by the US Department of Justice during the Obama administration revealed the overuse of expulsions and suspensions to discipline kids who live in poverty. Black, brown, Native American, and poor white children not only get suspended and expelled more often than middle-class or rich kids; they are also disciplined more harshly from kindergarten onward, and the police are called in more frequently. Incredibly, even five-year-olds have been handcuffed for having tantrums in school.

In the summer of 2018, I performed *Notes from the Field* at the Royal Court Theatre in London. There I learned that this is not only a US problem. Students in London are using what is called *subvertising*—that is, sending political messages in forms that resemble ads from well-known brands, such as posters in the London Undergound—to bring attention to the issue there. The ads ask for more financial support and more compassionate disciplinary practices. As in the US, a study at the University of Edinburgh revealed that, in the UK, students excluded from school by age twelve are four times more likely to be incarcerated as adults.

We are failing to meet the needs of our most vulnerable and troubled children. And this is a *choice*. Our policy choices as a society and our decisions about where to allocate resources—pouring them into prisons rather than into mental health or education—have turned our schools into a road to incarceration for too many of our youth. Because this is not only an American issue, we have an opportunity to invite new ideas, new ways of thinking about the disenfranchised.

In some ways, the current political climate is discouraging, but in other ways, I see room for hope. There is certainly a greater awareness now of these social injustices—and of the ability of ordinary people to do something about them. Some of the individuals represented in this play stand as an inspiring testament to that hope.

This is a time for people to cease being spectators and to instead be moved to get out there and do something to effect change. It is time to ask ourselves, "Who are we? What do we believe in? What kind of country do we want to be?"

I believe that art can inspire action. It can motivate us to reimagine a world where schools are more than sorting mechanisms for the haves and the have-nots, where they can function as centers for a *culture* of learning in which teachers, staff, administrators, parents, and students from all communities are respected and nurtured intellectually, physically, and creatively.

But that is a type of reimagining that needs to include all kinds of voices, especially those that have been historically discounted. It is a reimagining that requires courage, empathy, and action. And it has to start with listening.

PRODUCTION NOTES

Casting and Approach

This work was performed as a one-person show as a part of the author's ongoing *On the Road: A Search for American Character* series.

The objective of the On the Road series, in which this work is approximately the nineteenth play, is to absorb America "word for word" in the spirit of the nation's "more perfect union" objective.

The play can be performed with any number of actors. It is the author's intention that actors would portray characters outside of their own race, gender, age, and "type" within a diverse company of actors. Depending on available resources, this may or may not be possible or desired, in which case, artists are encouraged to cast and perform the play in any configuration of identity they deem meaningful or useful.

The author has often been asked in interviews if this work is mimicry or impressionism. It is not. Rather, when performed, it is a living document of speech in a moment and time in history. The actor is asked to take each real person at their word and with their word, to give full attention to their every utterance as recorded here.

Though it was not the case when the *On the Road* series began in the late 1970s, technology now affords artists working on the production the opportunity to see exactly who the people are and how they behave physically and linguistically. Actors are therefore encouraged, unless it is contrary to the director's vision, to use all available documentary footage of those represented in these pages in order to study their language and to use this study as another doorway into understanding and representing their identity.

Punctuation and Repetition

Punctuation is used to mark when speech starts and stops. Incomplete sentences and incomplete thoughts are intentional. Repeated words are intentional and should be spoken.

The Presence of the Interviewer

The interviewer's presence is always implied. The interviewer is the audience. A lot of the show is direct address to the audience, but the audience should be thought of as a single individual unless the character is specifically talking to a crowd.

The Slide

Slides with the character's name, their occupation or position, and a title of the piece that follows are a part of the play and a part of the text. It is sometimes useful to audiences to include the same information on an insert in the program. As the slides are essential to the audience's understanding of what they're watching, it is also helpful if the pedagogy of the slides is introduced once the house is opened. In that way, the audience will be primed to look at the slides in relationship to the performer. The slides and the information on the slides are an important guide.

Music

Marcus Shelby composed and performed live music onstage for performances of this play by Ms. Smith. Any genre of music and number of musicians can be employed, as this would be a directorial choice. The relationship between the performer and the musician was conceived by the author and created between the author/performer and the musician in the tradition of jazz and jazz improvisation. Hence, the onstage presence of a musician is intentional in this, the play's original form.

Helper

A nonspeaking helper is used in lieu of a stagehand. In the Second Stage Theater and American Repertory Theater productions, a twentysomething white male was the helper. As the helper is visible, and as race is both significant and movable in this and other works of Ms. Smith, selection of the nonspeaking helper's presence should be an aesthetic and perhaps sociological consideration.

The actor performs barefoot unless otherwise noted.

Speak the speech, I pray you, as I pronounced it to you, trippingly on the tongue; but if you mouth it, as many of our players do, I had as lief the town-crier spoke my lines. Nor do not saw the air too much with your hand, thus, but use all gently; for in the very torrent, tempest, and, as I may say, whirlwind of your passion, you must acquire and beget a temperance that may give it smoothness.

—WILLIAM SHAKESPEARE, *Hamlet*, act III, scene ii

[Slide]

In Memory of:

Anna Young Smith
1924–2003

and

Dr. Maxine Greene
1914–2014

and

Mr. Jonathan Demme
1944–2017

[Slide]

The material in this play is composed of verbatim excerpts from interviews conducted by Anna Deavere Smith unless otherwise noted.

These excerpts are drawn from a pool of 250 interviews conducted in four geographic areas of the United States and abroad.

ACT ONE

[Slide]

PROLOGUE

[Slide]

SHERRILYN IFILL

PRESIDENT AND DIRECTOR-COUNSEL
NAACP LEGAL DEFENSE AND EDUCATIONAL FUND
FROM AN ONSTAGE CONVERSATION BETWEEN MS. IFILL AND MS. SMITH
BALTIMORE, MARYLAND, JUNE 3, 2015

"Big Bets"

"Big Bets"

(Ms. Ifill is a public figure. Really good with a crowd, could run for office. African American, late forties. Brightly colored jacket, simple slacks. Footage is available to study her speech patterns, some of which are indicated within the text via punctuation.

In a theater in Baltimore, standing room only, a crowd that is really revved up, not that long after the Baltimore riots in 2015. Onstage being interviewed by the author. Handheld mic in her hand, easy chairs, table, flowers, water.)

I get asked this question all the time: what—how would you, what is the number one civil rights issue of the day. And . . . and I'm very uncomfortable with that question. Because . . . it is impossible to talk about the criminal justice system. Mass incarceration. Without talking about education. Because this country is always engaged in investments. *Big* investments, we make *big* bets. Nineteen-fifties, you know, this country massively invested in the creation of the suburbs, right? We created the interstate highway system. We provided, you know, tax credits to developers to build suburbs—that were racially exclusionary, by the way. But we made an investment! We decided—we—we made a massive investment in creating a middle class, *really* beginning in the 1930s, when the federal government started to insure mortgages, and *only* insured mortgages for—for white people, but we made an investment.

Now today, we pretend we don't make investments. 'Cause we talk about balancing the budget, and deficits. And we don't have any money, and we don't make—but we always make investments. And one of the *huge* investments that we made was in the criminal justice system. And that investment was made at the expense of other investments. We have taken dollars that we used to give, and that we could give, to invest in the issue of mental illness. It's not that we're *not* investing in mental illness. We are. We're investing it in the prison system. It's not that we're, you know, talking—we—we decided we're going to cut the budget and so we're not investing in education. Yeah. Kinda. We've taken it to the prison system.

So what we do is we take these investments that we *could* make, these big bets, and we place them somewhere. And that's what we call policy. Which, you know, makes people's *eyes* glaze over, but we should understand; policy is made up of the investments that we as a society decide to make.

The moment that we're in, by the way. Not only, you know, [here] in Baltimore. [I] spent time in St. Louis County, with Ferguson over the last year, and our lawyers were down North Charleston, in South Carolina. Where Walter Scott was killed, and the man we saw on the video. Being shot.

There's a lot of heaviness in this country in this moment. There's a lot of pain. And, you know, I always say, "America is an interesting place." It's like one of my favorite movies, *The Matrix*. Where, you know, every once and a while, you eat the red pill? Whatever is the pill that makes you see the matrix. But you know, we can't sustain it. Because it's awful! You know, when you see all the strings, and you see everything that's behind the scenes. We *do* have to enjoy ourselves. And live, and . . . make a way, you know, out of no way. But sometimes, you—you *have* to have these moments if we are going to move our society forward. It takes moments, kind of—almost epic moments. To *move* us, to be able to take the red pill. So there's a way in which we are confronting this moment. And there is a privilege in that confrontation.

THE DEATH OF FREDDIE GRAY

Actual newsclips about Freddie Gray's arrest and death (April 2015 in Balti-more, Maryland) are shown.

LESTER HOLT: Good evening. Baltimore police are the latest to fall under the harsh national spotlight over the death of a suspect. A short time ago, officials there released security video of the arrest of a twenty-five-year-old man whose death from a partially severed spine has raised questions about police actions. (*Screams are heard.*) Cell phone video shows twenty-five-year-old Freddie Gray being taken into custody and placed in a police van a week ago. Some time between this moment and his arrival at the police precinct, Gray's spine was nearly severed. But tonight, police still can't say how Gray died yesterday.

[Slide]

KEVIN MOORE

VIDEOGRAPHER OF THE BEATING OF FREDDIE GRAY
DELI WORKER
BALTIMORE, MARYLAND

"Just a Glance"

"Just a Glance"

(*A very tall [six-foot-three or so] charismatic, handsome black man in his late twenties, early thirties. Wears an oversize hoodie, with letters spelling* COPWATCH. *He carries a cell phone and a small camera, visible or nearly visible at all times. Think gun in a holster. West Baltimore accent.*

Walking past the very housing project where Freddie Gray was killed—graffiti and a beautiful mural commemorating Freddie where he actually died, showing the interviewer/audience, author around the neighborhood. He is talking directly to a videographer who is in front of his face somehow always. Live video of the actor as Kevin is projected behind the action. Cars slow down as they pass him and he acknowledges them with a nod.)

The screams [are] what woke me out my *sleep*. The *screamin'*. I'm like, well, "What's all this screaming?" And then they came to pull me up, like, "Dude, they tasin' him, they tasin' him!" I'm like, "Wooh!" (*High-pitched.*) So I jumped up and threw some clothes on and went out to see what was going on, you know. And then I came out that way, and I'm like, "Holy shit!" You know what I'm saying?

They had him all bent up and he was handcuffed and, like, facedown on his stomach. But they had the—the heels of his *feet* like almost in his back? And he was handcuffed at the time. And they had the knee in the neck, and that pretty much explains the three cracked vertebrae and crushed lernix [*pronounciation of* larynx], 80 percent of his spinal cord being severed and stuff. And then when they picked him up, I had to zoom in to get a closer look on his face. You could see the *pain* in his face, you know what I'm saying? But then they pulled around on Mount Street and pulled him out *again*! To put leg shackles on him. You put leg shackles on a man that could barely walk to the paddy wagon? That doesn't make sense to me. And I've never known a-a-a on-the-beat officer to carry leg shackles in—on their person or in the van, that's something that you do when you're going to another compound or when you're being transported to the court or something like that. They don't put leg shackles on you outside, they just don't do it! You know, so you put leg shackles on a man that can't walk. You know. Then you toss him in the back of the paddy wagon like a dead animal. You know what I'm saying? Then you don't even put a seat belt on him. So basically, he's handcuffed, shackled, sliding back and forth in a steel cage, basically. 'Cause that's what—it's not *padded* back there. I don't know why everybody seems to say, "Oh, oh, uh, it's a pad—it's padded." *No*, it's not padded. It's about—it's—it's about as padded as that v—the outside of that van.

It's *ridiculous* how bad they hurt that man. I mean, come on, a crushed lernix? Can you do that to yourself? Three cracked vertebrae? Can you do that to yourself? Can you sever 80 percent of your own spinal cord? You know what I'm saying? In the back of a paddy wagon, shackled and handcuffed, no less? I wish you could just see how they had him. So I'm like, "Man, this shit is just crazy, man. They just don't care anymore!" Man, I just feel like we need to *record* it, you know'm saying? We need to get this word out that this thing is—is happening. This is the only weapon that we *have* that's actually . . . the camera's the only thing that we have that can actually protect us, that's *not* illegal, you know what I'm saying? But in—in the same sense, these guys could feel threatened or, "Oh, well, I mistook this camera for a gun." You know what I'm saying? So that's what I'm sayin'! [Like I said,] I haven't really filmed anything before, or been known for filmin', you know what I'm saying?

But *that* time I was like, man, "Somebody has to *see* this." You know what I mean? "I have to *film* this." When I touched back down around, I just basically called every news station that I could and just got the video out there! You know, mainstream, thirteen, forty-five, uh, eleven, *New York* Times, *Russia Today.* (*Laughs.*) I don't even speak *Russian* but, you know, I did the interview.

(*Answering a question.*) No, it was actually [I took it with] my phone! (*Laughs.*) And . . . I had some brothers from Ferguson, and they came out and supported me. Yeah, and they actually spent the night at my house! My brothers from Ferguson, they took me to *Best* Buy. And brought me four cameras. Basically *arming* me! It's a movement. It's not gonna stop here.

(*Answering a question.*) Eye contact. *This* story [of Freddie Gray's eye contact] was with the—the *whole story* since it be— since it happened. That's how the officers, I guess, wrote the paperwork: That [Freddie] made eye contact. And he looked suspicious. Oh. "And that gave us probable cause to" . . . do whatever. We know the truth, y'know what I'm saying? Just a glance. The eye contact thing, that—it—it—it—it—sets off, it's like a trigger. That's all it takes here in Baltimore, is just a glance.

(*He sits down somewhere—a step, the curb, a box. He starts to cry.*)

Have you ever been to a place where (*six-second pause*) you don't *feel* tired—you *tired* of being tired. You know'm saying? Where you *fed* up. And it's nothing else left. And you can't get any lower? (*He listens to an answer.*) *Past* that. You know? So . . . That's where I've been. (*He listens to a question.*)

Gotta keep climbing. You gotta keep fightin'. You gotta keep climbing. You gotta keep praying. You gotta keep doing all'v the things that you know can make you stronger because in the end (*a deep inward breath*), you just gonna need all the strength that you can muster to git yourself from that hole, it's like a bunch of crabs trying to pull you back. You know what I'm saying? It's like *quicksand*. And you fighting and you fighting you just sinking faster and faster. You know.

And I hate it that Baltimore is going through *such* harsh times right now. The fact that my children might have to fight this fight, you know? I'm not gonna be here forever. You know'm saying? Then how do I train my children to deal with this, you know what I'm saying?

(*He stands up, listens to a question from the interviewer/audience.*)

The leaders? Right now, man, the leaders are looking pretty assholeish. Uh. Look. It's—it's just so much the leaders can do. You know what I'm sayin'? It's only so mu—so much they can say. But at the end of the day the leaders gonna make up their minds. They're gonna *do* what they wanna *do*, you know what'm saying, so . . . we have to make it better, not wait *around* for *them* to make it better. These people are *tired* and—and—and they want *answers*. And it seems like the only way they can get answers, to them, is if they cost the city money!

Actual newsclips of Allen Bullock smashing a Baltimore city police car on April 25, 2015, are shown.

[Slide]

ALLEN BULLOCK

PROTESTER
BALTIMORE, MARYLAND

"Runnin' from 'Em"

"Runnin' from 'Em"

(*An eighteen-year-old black man. Lean. Wiry. Not that long ago he was a "shorty," and you can still see it in his face and demeanor. In contrast to the sagging pants, etc., in the video, his clothing looks like it just came out of the laundry. Simple white T-shirt, khaki pants. New-looking boots or sneakers of the time period.*

Well-appointed lawyer's office, downtown Baltimore, upper floor with a panoramic view of the city. Very large chair, gives impression of a throne. Hand gestures of the time, probably specific to Baltimore. He is looking out the window at the horizon; sometimes almost turns his back to the interviewer/audience. The feeling is that he couldn't care less about the interviewer, almost like we are wasting his time.)

I don't even look the police way, tell you the truth, that's not even me, like . . . I don't even pay the police no mind, like they look at me, I turn my head, I look ba— If I'm gonna look back at you, I'm not gonna mug you, I'ma just look away, you feel me? That's all it is to—

Because if you look at a police so hard or so straight—I don't know, like see how he was, Freddie Gray, you feel me, <u>in</u> the <u>way</u>, like he was around this neighborhood, if the neighborhood police they don't <u>care</u>, they—do—not care bout <u>none o' that</u> you— if they *know* you in that neighborhood, they gonna *do* some t'— I don't care what neighborhood you in, it could be a quiet neighborhood, anything, the police know, you from . . . *bein' bad*, or not even bein' bad, but bein' around the area, anything, hanging with somebody, that that they know, that's bad, they gonna *harass* you—and if they gon' harass you— "Why you lookin' at me like that?"— They will *ask* you "Why you looking at me like that," like, in a <u>smart</u> way you feel me jump out the car, pulling their stick, all that, you feel me.

I had a police ask me why'm I walkin' in the street, why am I *crossin'* in the street, like.

"Whatchu <u>mean</u> why am I crossin' in the street?" I'm saying something back he jumpin' outta the car, so I get back on the curb. You feel me there's no need for you to get outta the car, and you feel me and talk at me, you could see why am I walking across the street. They don't say, ask you, me—"Sir, come here," nunna that, you just . . . ask me why am I walkin' across the street, y'feel me. It's not uh late outside, it's not nunnathat so what is you . . . I don't know there's just a lotta police out here thisss . . . bein' police bein what they do.

(*He listens to a question and for the first time faces the interviewer/audience.*)

Be smart, that's what I would gotta say to you, be smart. Thass all 'ass 'sall is *to* it, if you know you . . . say if you—I don't care whatchu do out there, that's your hustle, if you got something on you, don't even pay the police no *mind,* y'feel, don't even draw no <u>attention</u>, but you not doing nut'in I *still* don't expect for you to draw no attention to the police, like, the police, out here, don't care, even if you don't got nuttin' *on* you! Why look at the police you ain't got no— Why mug the police? You feel me? No reason at <u>all</u>, so I wouldn't even pay the police no *mind,* I don't <u>pay</u> the police out here no mind. They <u>mug</u> me all day, I don't care about nunnathat they doin' like—I *see* 'em, you feel me, like, I don't say too much stuff the police an' all that like for *no reason at all,* like . . .

(*Pause.*)

I'm just sayin' that like I'm out here in these streets.

(He looks back out the window at the horizon. The interviewer asks another question. He looks back in their direction but looks down at his arm, examining it quickly as he speaks.)

I got beat. It only happen— It happen—'bout four times, I— Four times, that's what I remember, four times.

(Another question, and he looks around randomly but not at the interviewer/audience. Perhaps he yawns.)

Runnin' from 'em, that's mostly what they—thass *all* they *can* beat me for, runnin' from 'em. The don't like it when you run from 'em.

It's a lotta people out here bein' harassed, gittin' killt, you fill me like. It ain't just cuz of no Freddie Gray got killt, people die every day. Police—you feel me, harass people, beat people every day.

(Another question, looking perhaps out the window, perhaps down at his feet, just not at the interviewer/audience.)

The stick—they use a what's name . . . Uhm, I forget what kinda stick it is. Sometimes they use their *hands.*

(Another question. He faces the interviewer/audience dead-on.)

You can't protect yourself! When it come to the police, you can't say too much, but run your mouth and once they see you really runnin' your mouth they try catch you or try do somethin' to you, an' 'specially if they ain't got no reason y'feelme to touch you, they def'nitley wanna touch you, like, they chase you all this 'n' you ain't got nuttin' on you, an they just chasin' you? Man they they worth ih—gonna make it worth they while, they gonna find, they gonna, not even put nuffin' on you they gonna *beat*chu.

Straight like that, it ain't no "Oh, I'm o' plant somethin' on him, they just do they wanna *do*, at that time, at that moment.

(Now he emphatically "schools" the interviewer/audience, straight on, direct, and gets more and more excited and more and more

direct. His appetite for talking is now sparked. He gets very upset and emphatic.)

It don't— It don't even matter this, at *this* point. I don't— It don't even *matter* if they black or white. I never s— I don't even— It ain't no black-or-white situation, I ain't tryin' to hear that. I done seen *plenny* o' police off [officers] do it, an' <u>I'm</u> black you feel me, *to* black people, an' I done seen plenny o' whi' [white] police do it, I done seen 'em do it together, it ain't no no no racist thing, ih— That's what I, I don't see no racist thing come into play.

I think issa *hatred* thing, like, they hate, you feel me like. If I ca—if you can't find nuttin' on *me* what's the whole point o' you lockin' me up or you beatin' me up, you feh [feel] me? For no reason, cuz I made you run? Come on now, like, you train to do this like . . .

'N' I could be runnin' for <u>no reason</u> juss for the police d'you feel me. If you mess wit me—why <u>mess</u> wit me y'feel me—'n' I'm gonna make you *mad*. Becuz you shouldneev' be *'arrasin'* me for *no reason* you feel m— I don't have no—nuffin' on me! You feel me—they—jumpin' outta the car, tryin'— "What? I'm gone! I'm running from you!"

(*Leaning forward toward the interviewer/audience.*)

I never got locked up nunnaduh time I get beat up, you feel me, cuz they don't find nuttin' on me nunnadat, I don't throw nothin' you feel me, nunnadat. They don't even . . .

(*Pause.*)

I really don't know. Thass all it is to it. Hey. Stuff happen erry day on Ballamaw City.

(*Looking out the window again.*)

ARRISON BRYANT

OUNDER OF EMPOWERMENT TEMPLE AME CHURCH
RMON AT FREDDIE GRAY'S FUNERAL
ARYLAND, APRIL 27, 2015

he Box"

"Breaking the Box"

(The video is actual footage of the funeral. Dignitaries including Jesse Jackson are behind the pulpit. A packed megachurch. Casket, lines of people paying respects. Hymn: "Pass Me Not, O Gentle Savior." Magnificent choir. Responsive church, babies crying, etc., individual calls building until a point when they join Bryant in the call "No justice! No peace." Bryant is GQ dapper, probably one of the best-dressed men in America. A brilliant preacher, both in terms of writing and delivery. Pastor Bryant is well-represented online for study of his preaching technique. The entire sermon, as well as many other sermons of his, are also available online for study.)

The Families United 4 Justice, they drove through the night, from New York, to be here. I want you to know who is with us. I'm thankful for the daughter of Eric Garner, who is here with us. The mother of Amadou Diallo is here with us. The mother of Kimani Gray is here with us. The sister of Shantel Davis is here with us. The mother of Ramarley Graham is here with us. The niece of Alberta Spruill is here with us. For *all* of them, would you give God a handclap of praise? Thank you so much for coming.

Would you find your way to Luke, chapter 7. Luke, chapter 7. I want to illuminate for your understanding verses 11 through 15. "Soon afterward, Jesus went to a town called Naim, and his disciples and a large crowd went along with him. As he approached the town gate, a dead boy was being carried out. The only son of his mother. And she was a widow. And a large crowd from the town was *with* her. And when the Lord saw her, His heart went out and He said, 'Don't cry.' Then he went up and touched the coffin. And those carrying it stood still. He said, 'Young man, I say to you, get up!' And the dead man sat up. And begin to talk. And Jesus gave him back to his mother."

[I] wanna preach for a little while tonight—today, using as a subject "Breaking the Box." Breaking the box.

One of the greatest tragedies in life is to think that you are free, but to still be confined to a box. Living in a box of stereotypes. Other people's opinion. Sweeping generalizations. And racial profiling. Sociologists have unearthed a newfound phenomenon called quarter-life crisis. And it says that this generation of youth in their mid-twenties begin meandering through the painstaking task of asking themselves, "What am I gonna do with my life? Is there any hope for me? What should I have done differently?"

(*Looking out into the congregation, specifically to one person.*)

Grandmother, I need you to know that Freddie *had* to have been in a quarter-midlife crisis. 'Cause at twenty-five years of age, being black in Baltimore, no opportunities to go to Johns Hopkins. No doors open at the University of Maryland. No scholarship to Morgan and no access to Coppin. "In a place where I have minimal opportunities," Freddie had to have asked, "when I can walk down the harbor and see Exelon, Under Armour—when it is that I can look across the water and see millions of dollars poured into Camden Yards and M&T Stadium." He had to have been asking himself, "*What* am I gonna do with my life?" He had to feel almost like he was boxed in.

Now, on April the twelfth at 8:39 in the morning, four officers on bicycles saw your son. And your son, in a subtlety of revolutionary stance, did something that black men were trained to—taught—know *not* to do. He looked police in the eye.

I want to tell this grieving mother, you are not burying a boy, you are burying a grown man. Who knew that one of the principles of being a man is looking somebody in the eye.

At 8:40, your son began running from the police. He began running. At 8:41, according to the timeline, he stopped. He stopped *not* because he was out of breath. He stopped *not* because he was a weakling. He stopped *not* because asthma had kicked in. He stopped because somewhere within the inner recesses of his own mind, he made up in his mind: "I'm tired of living in a box." And so he *stopped* running.

So as we jaywalk in our text, we notice that Jesus and his disciples are coming to an unknown hamlet of a town known Naim. And Jesus is overwhelmed by this crowd, and—and he stops as he's seeing the funeral processional. Jesus says to this mother, "Don't cry. Whatever you do, don't cry." It's a *strange* prescription to tell a family in pain. "Don't cry." When the Bible declares that weeping may endure for a night and joy comes in the morning, He says to the mother, "Don't cry." But I came to tell this grandmother. I came to tell the aunt. I came to tell Freddie Sr. I came to tell Freddie's five sisters, "Don't cry." And the *reason* why I want you not to cry is because Freddie's death is not in vain.

After this day, we gonna *keep on* marching. After this day, we gonna keep demanding justice. After this day, we gonna keep *exposing* a culture of corruption. After *this day*, we gonna keep monitoring our own neighborhood. *Whatever* you do, don't cry!

Amazingly! Jesus does something: he lifts up his hand. And he changes the position of healing. Every other time Jesus has healed, it has always been a lateral move: he would reach his hand out. But when we find ourselves in this narrative for the very first time in sacred scripture, Jesus lifts his hands up. And when he lifts his hands up, he touches the casket.

And I'm praying to God that God will lay his hand on everything that's been trying to keep black people in a box . . . I don't know whether I'm talking about redlining of zip codes or gentri-fication or whether I'm talking about a prison pipeline or inad-equate public schools, but whatever box that has been placed around the life and the future of young black babies in this city, I'm praying: *God*, put your *hand* on the box!

He said—watch this—to the young man *in* the box still, "Get up."

This is not the time for us as a people to be sitting on the cor-ner drinking malt liquor! This is not the time for us to be playing lottery or to be at the Horseshoe Casino! This is not the time for us to be walking around with our pants hanging down past our behind! This is not the time for us to have no respect for our legacy and for our history! This is not the time for tattoos all over your neck! He said, "I need you to get up." In spite of the fact that they spend more money on special education than they do on gifted and talented programs—get yourself up! In spite of what they told you [that] you oughtta be and what you are gonna become: get up! You are not Lil Wayne, you are *not* Lil Boosie. You are in the mantle and the legacy of Thurgood Marshall and Clarence Mitchell Sr. and Parren Mitchell and Kweisi Mfume! Get your black self up and *change* this city!

I don't know what Jesus *you* serve. But the Jesus *I* serve is not blond and blue-eyed. The Jesus *I* serve looked just like Freddie Gray. And that Jesus is the Jesus who will lift us up again.

He speaks to him. And He says to this young man, "Get up." And He never opens the casket. You miss what I just said? He tells the young man, "Get UP." When he's in a *closed* casket! He was sending a message to Black America. Don't expect nobody to open the door for you! If they don't open the door, kick that sucker down and get what you need! GIT UP!!!!

The young man got up. When he was supposed to be dead; supposed to be over. And he got up without any prompting, ladies and gentlemen. And he started talking.

I don't know how you can be black in America and be silent. With everything that we dealing with—with our children being gunned down in the streets!

Freddie—Freddie, just like this boy in Luke chapter 7, he broke outta the box. And again, Luke the gospel writer and physician has let me down. Because when the boy broke outta the box, he forgot to tell me what that boy said. Gettin' out of the casket! But if you'll allow me to validate my sanctified imagination: When that black boy got outta the casket, do you wanna know what he said? He said, "No justice!" (*Audience: "No peace!"*) "No justice!" (*Audience: "No peace!"*) "No justice!" (*Audience: "No peace!"*)

Actual documentary footage is shown on the video screen. Excerpts of coverage of the trials of the officers involved in Gray's death are shown. Then we hear the voice of State's Attorney for Baltimore, Marilyn Mosby.

"I have heard your calls for 'No justice, no peace.' However, your peace is sincerely needed as I work to deliver justice on behalf of Freddie Gray. To the rank and file officers of the Baltimore Police Department, please know that these accusations against these six officers are not an indictment on the entire force. I come from five generations of law enforcement. My father was an officer. My mother was an officer. Several of my aunts and uncles, my recently departed and beloved grandfather—"

The video is cut off as a musician is revealed playing a riff. (All previous productions used an African American male in his forties, a jazz bass player.)

The musician is playing a riff on "Spanish Harlem" by Jerry Leiber and Phil Spector. We hear a recording of a woman, Alicia Keys, speaking lyrics from "The Rose That Grew from Concrete" by Tupac Shakur.

Did you hear about the rose that grew from a crack in the concrete?
Proving nature's laws wrong, it learned how to walk without having
*   feet*
Funny it seems but by keeping its dreams
It learned to breathe fresh air
Long live the rose that grew from concrete
When no one else even cared
No one else even cared

THE ROSE IN CONCRETE

MICHAEL TUBBS

COUNCILMAN, SUBSEQUENTLY MAYOR OF STOCKTON, CALIFORNIA

"Tupac"

"Tupac"

(At the time of the interview, Tubbs was the youngest city councilman Stockton, and possibly California, ever had. Tall, lanky, a boyish smile and face. Research can be done to find clips of him on television shows. He wears a suit, sports shirt, oxfords.

He and the musician give each other high fives. Tubbs speaks very quickly, like a small boat zooming across water. Sometimes minor prepositions or other small words are inaudible. It's a bit of a verbal feat to keep the monologue moving along quickly. Stanford grad, none of the affectations of most current Ivy League grads. A politician but still fresh. Almost disarmingly open and vulnerable in his manner.)

So what I would say about Stockton: Stockton's really ground zero for a lot of issues facing America. My aspirations right now? You're gonna laugh—they're really simple. I just want a grocery store in my district? There's no grocery store. I had no idea. I don't eat really healthy. My girlfriend, now my wife, is a vegetarian. And she went to Stanford. And she came to live with me [for] like a week. And she was, like, breaking *out*. She's like, "Michael, I just want an apple. Where can I get an apple?" And I couldn't think of where to get her an apple. I said, "I don't know. Where can I get you an apple from?" It was about twenty minutes away. So that really prompted me: "Okay, let's do something about that."

We're doing some work around boys and men of color alliances, so we can figure out how to improve outcomes for boys and men of color. For a lot of young people in—in Stockton? There's almost this prevailing sense of nihilism? And I'm not sure it's peculiar to Stockton? I think in any community where you have segregation along race and class, you have a undercaste of—of young people, who just feel forgotten, neglected, and are just angry and don't know what to be angry at. It's—it's—I think they understand there's some things structurally wrong. But they haven't been taught what that is, so oftentimes it—it manifests itself in self-blame. Or—or, "It's our fault," or—or "I need to work harder." When often, when that—part of that's true, but oftentimes there are real structural forces keeping—keeping some people down, so I think, for young people in Stockton, there's almost a sense of nihilism. There's a sense of leveled aspiration. In terms of not being exposed to everything that's out here. But it's also this amazing resilience. Whenever I—whenever I talk to young people in Stockton, I always quote the Tupac poem, about the rose that grew from concrete? When he talks about "Long live the rose that grew from concrete / when no one else cares," and I think that really, really illustrates the young people in my opinion—Stockton—the—these young people, who are *growing* in cracks of concrete, not in soil, but in—but in concrete. Where they're not supposed to grow. And sometimes they come out with a little bit of *scars*, sometimes they come out with—with a couple petals not—that are not perfectly right. But the fact that they're growing and trying to thrive in—in their community with so many problems, to me, is inspiring.

I'm sorry, I always talk in stories; they really illustrate points.

When I was on the campaign trail, I was reading to [a] group of *first* graders. And I was reading about Dr. Martin Luther King Jr., and I got to the part where he was assassinated, so I tried to go through the page really quickly, 'cause I didn't want to talk to, like, six-year-olds about death. So I tried to turn quickly, but one boy said, "Wait, Mr. Tubbs! My uncle got shot." And he said it so matter-of-factly, I thought his uncle lived, so I'm like, "Oh my gosh, I'm so sorry, I'm glad he's still here with us now." He said, "Oh no, he died." (*Dead stop.*) And then another little boy was like, "Mr. Tubbs, my *cousin* got shot!" And then before—then before I could turn the page, every student in that classroom knew somebody that had been shot or was a victim of a violent death.

These are first graders, six years old. I remember looking at the teacher, and she was tearing up, I—I—*she* was tearing up, I was tearing up, and I think that really illustrates some of why— why nihilism and trauma and violence is just so routine and so normal that a six-year-old can look you in your eye and say, "My uncle died," and say it so matter-of-factly. At six years old. What happens at seven, eight, nine, ten?

Young people aren't dumb, they—they might not have the fancy academic language, but they know that there's not much opportunity. They know they go to schools where it's a big deal to go to college? They—they know that there's—they know there's not a whole bunch of private-sector employment in this city, so they—might [not] know [how] to describe these things, and they may say things like, "Oh, ain't nothing for—ain't nothing for me to do," or "There's nothing for us." And they may [not] say it in that way, but they understand that something structurally is wrong.

I think that leads you just to nihilism and it's—especially around our young *men*, which is a—not for all of them, but for the population that's been the most vulnerable, and the—the dropouts, and those [that] are in the pipeline, and those that are . . . killing each other, it's just this idea that my—the value of life, like, my life doesn't matter, what—what—what life is this where I'm struggling to eat every day? What life is this when I can't see— Like, I talk to *young* people—I'm like, "Okay, where you wanna go to college?" and they're like, "I can't see past *eighteen, realistically*!" And like, "No, I want you to sit down and write down your dreams, I just want you to— What's your goal?" "I just want to be alive by twenty-five."

It's heartbreaking, so. In that way, I think, that's how the nihilism will manifest itself. Prison or—or death. There's really no other alternatives or options for our boys and men of color in Stockton. Prison or death.

ON THE RIVER

[Slide]

TAOS PROCTOR

YUROK FISHERMAN/FORMER INMATE
YUROK TRIBAL RESERVATION
KLAMATH, CALIFORNIA

"The Baddest"

"The Baddest"

(Yurok Reservation. A salmon-fishing tribe. Standing in a fishing boat at the mouth of the Klamath River exactly where it joins the Pacific Ocean. August, height of fishing season. Taos wears orange fishing waders. He's about six-foot-four or taller, almost three hundred pounds. Tattoos. A disquieting moment of silence as he surveys the entire audience and looks off at the grandeur of the river. The first of all the speakers to take the time to do this. At first, it seems not entirely welcoming. A sense that you come to him. He doesn't come to you. Once he starts speaking, there's generosity in what he shares. However, there's always a sense that he is watching us as intently as we are watching him. Actual Yurok ceremonial song is in the background. The musician onstage improvises with the ceremonial song.)

I got to about the <u>eighth</u> grade. Well, I, I didn't leave; they kicked me out. Well, I got in too many fights and it was always my fault from the teachers, and well—well—well, beginning, since I was a kid, I have to say, I went to school, and I was always getting in trouble, got kicked out, and then they said I hit the teacher, so I got kicked out of, like, Redwood School, out in Smith River. Well, I just pulled away from her, and it hurt her arm or something. I was a little kid, probably about eight? So they kicked me oudda that school 'n' then I went to Pine <u>Grove</u> School 'n' then I was always just in the office or sitting there because of getting in trouble. So I got kicked outta there, and I went to—then I—then I went to Crescent Elk I got kicked out of there. And then I went to community school by the juvenile hall. And when I went there, then, I really didn't git kicked oudda <u>there</u>, they just threw me in juvenile hall. But I learned howda read in juvenile hall. I learned howda read. And then and then I was too bad there, y'know? Fightin' 'n' arguin' 'n' 'n' not doin' mah work so then they put me in the probation office. With the probation officers. And then . . . then they tried to put me back in high school after I's tryin' da start doin' good, put me back in high school I got kicked oudda there, 'n' then I went to prison. CYA 'n' prison. California Youth Authority. Yeah, I was the first one of my friends to go to CYA, first one to go to prison.

(*He listens to a question, thinks, looks us in the eye, steady, then:*)

'Cause they know I'm a killer.

(*Pause.*)

(*Raucous laughter.*)

No. I had the mentality I was gonna be the worstest and the baddest. 'Cause I'm the baddest of the *bad*!

Whatever I do in life, I try to do it to the—to, like, the best of my ability? I'm gonna have more drugs than anyone. I'm gonna— I'm gonna—I'm gonna have *cars*? I'z nineteen when I went to y'know San Quentin. I was moved around prison prison prison. Yeah, San Quentin, High Desert, uh, Pleasant Valley, Avenal. Well, well I started out at the like the lowest . . . the lowest level of prison. I start out at Avenal at like level one er two, and then, I paroled from High Desert, High Desert, um . . . C Yard (*a beat*) shoe kick out. So uh, I, I'z bad through prison too. Probably my fights got me moved around.

Prison fights? Just any kind o' disrespect. If somebody even looks at you a lil' bit funny, then you might hafta just sock 'em up. Usually it's a word kicks it off. *Punk, butch, lame* . . . Some talking 'bout yer family, some talkin' 'bout yer race. A lot of people din't like Native Americans. Iss like . . . just looked down upon, y'know? I went to school Crescent City there ain' no Native Americans! It's just probly much just the whole class w'be like twenny-sumpthin' kinds, 'n' I'd be like one er two of us in there. And then you wouldn't talk to the other Native Americans.

(*Considering a question.*)

Cause you wouldn't wanna be ya know— (*Burst of laughter.*) Be th'only Native American talkin' to a Native American. Kinda! All white people! Maybe a Mexican here and there? The be no black people, no black people. Thiz 'n' black people Crescent City when I was growin up.

(*He looks at the musician.*)

I-I-I was wondering—a was wonderin' y'know? How they keep 'em out. I seen black people on TV.

Prison don't do nothing but make you a worser person. Made me where I didn't care if I hurt someone. . . . And the longer you stay in prison, the more you lose your feelings about even *caring*. You don't care if you stab someone. You just stab 'em 'n' stab'm five or ten time, you don't care. Who cares? I mean, they're worthless! Or beat 'em up. You don't care. Knock their teeth out. You don't care. I mean, I didn't care if a person had life. I'd walk up and sock 'em in the head.

Everyone's *bad* in there, it . . . don't really matter what you do, to a person that's there for twenty-five to life. I did everything I could to stay on top of the food chain. I did day for day in prison because of my fighting. Mean' I come out my cell and I make the whole yard lay down? Put down the whole yard. Lay it down! You git in a fight and then everyone has to lay down while you're fighting cuz eh gunners gonna shoot. I didn't care if they shot in the yard. I ain't give a shit. I'm doing it and I'm gonna make it happen and I'm gonna do what it *does*. That world, that world in prison is just as strong as the world out here, 'cept for you're in a cage. Sure, people get hurt; people get stabbed. You can do anything you want, you know what I mean?

That's why I—I can't get the school thing. I was the top of everything, everywhere, in my whole life. I'm the best at everything I'm doing. If I'm on the river, I'm the best at everything I'm gonna do. I started a *business* at being the best. I'm the best at smoked [fish]. I'm the baddest there is. 'Cause I'm the baddest of the *bad*! Y'know what I mean? And when I got to, y'know, prison, it was the same thing. I— It's actually like a big game in there, y'know [what] I mean? I mean, I got stabbed like ten times, but it don't matter.

(*He looks at someone in the audience as if to hear a question.*)

Rape? (*Loud burst of laughter.*) I'm—I'm almost six-four, almost three hundred pounds, I don't think no one's gonna try to rape me! Can't rape the willing. (*Loud laughter.*) I can't say nothing about that. Never been raped. I mean, it's not . . . It's bad if someone *does* get raped, you know? But . . . I mean, *I* never raped no one. I mean, I guess, uh, I guess stab 'em? Stab someone if they try to rape you? That's how I'd do it if you're gonna be scared and—and—and cr— whine and crybaby and that, then sure, you're gonna get abused and treated bad. But if you just go out there and you're just a monster, then you're gonna—you're gonna just be a monster!

I mean, like, talking about it makes me go back to a bad place that—yeah, yeah, I'm in—I'm in a happy spot now, you know what I mean? And . . . yeah. Just thinking about all the badness— Now that I cleaned up my life, I'm doing very well with everything. I got a family, too. I got a kid. He's wonderful, ain't he. Shaqoon. Call him Hog.

He—he—he's perfect. (*Dead stop.*) Where you gonna be at later? I can get you a fish and some smoked salmon.

(*Very long pause as he stares into the audience, listening.*)

When I look in the mirror? I see a very good person that's just been down a rough road. And I don't know if it was my schooling or—or—or growing up where I grew up, or what it was, that put me on this road? But I wouldn't change this road for nothing? Because this is the road that made me who I am? And got me to where I'm at. I didn't know I was on the rough road, I always just—I always just thought: life's hard, you know?

[Slide]

JUDGE ABBY ABINANTI

CHIEF JUDGE, YUROK TRIBAL COURT
SAN FRANCISCO AND KLAMATH, CALIFORNIA

"Broken"

"Broken"

(*In a straightbacked chair on her porch, on a hill directly over the mouth of the Klamath River and the Pacific Ocean. In her sixties. A fantastic-looking person; takes-your-breath-away type. Charismatic. There's a lot of story in her sheer presence. Cool, tall, lean. Cowboy boots, long gray hair, silver and turquoise rings. Soft-spoken. Very rarely looks at the interviewer/audience, up into the sky, off to the horizon, sometimes turns all the way around and looks down at the river and ocean. Musician onstage, underscoring the monologue.*)

Taos. He's in our tribe. Part of it is just he's very big, and he . . . acted out. He did things in school that he probably shouldn't have and nobody stopped to say, "Taos, what's wrong? Why are you doing this?" And now that he's out, y' know, when he does wrong by *me*, then I help sit him down and I'll go, "Why are you doing this, Taos? We need to figure this out, because you're gonna get in trouble. If you go away, who's gonna tend to *your* family's graves? Who's gonna raise your *son*?"

You cannot deal with children if you don't have a sense of kindness and respect. And if you don't like them. And if you *don't* have a system that supports them and likes them and stays with 'em. I get mad at you so I throw you outta school? What is—what is *that*? NO. I get mad at you so we need to come *closer*. You did something <u>wrong</u>: so you need to come <u>closer</u> you don't need to go <u>further</u>. You know, if I have something to offer, then you need to be *close*, you don't need to be further.

Y'know, we believe you *get* things from your ancestors. [When

I was a kid] the old people used to *laugh* around and say, "Oh, you are just like your grandfather." Meaning my attitude. Now, my grandfather was shot down as a bank robber, and he *did* kill white people, and he did do those things and he didn't take to the reservation life very well. You have to learn the wisdom with it. I was in a *fist*fight and somebody *clobbered* me. And they were saying, "Say 'I give up,' or say 'Uncle.' " And this other person walked by and said, "You may as well kill her, 'cause she'll never say it." And it's true!

You cannot fistfight everybody. You know, you just can't. It doesn't mean you can't *fight*. It means you have to *measure* how to do it. 'Mean, I gave up fistfighting at some <u>point</u>. You know and then I learned to do *this*. I learned the law; this is what I can do. [I fought a] sufficient amount. But I think you get to a place and you go, "You gotta look at this man." You know, and . . . "At your weight class and whatever. You're gonna get your butt kicked!" You *can't* be like my grandfather. You *can't* be shooting people down. You *can't* be stealing their money. 'Cause it makes 'em nuts.

School-to-prison pipeline? I think the kids are—are not finishing school, they can't get jobs, then they end up trying to make do, and they end up going to jail! I mean, that's what it is.

Some of it's school discipline. We don't have good relationships with these people. (*Pause.*) Educators. (*Pause.*) White people. They identify our [tribal] kids as having behavioral *issues*. So then they get suspended from school. Then they get arrested at school. Y'know, we had an eight-year-old in Klamath who they were about to put cuffs on, and I sent people over there to stop it. You can<u>not</u> cuff an eight-year-old! It's stupid! If . . . if you have children who are suffering to the extent that they act out in schools and do things they should not do . . . that could include hitting another child, hitting a teacher, having some kind of *fit*—and then they get expelled from school, then they get *mad* at somebody or they attack a school resource officer, then they get *handcuffed*, then they go to *jail* or *probation* or juvenile *hall*, and then it just goes from there and it—it just keeps *going*! And nobody says, "*Why is this kid like this?*" Y'know? "*What happened?*" You know, I mean, *come on*, you know? You know, that kinda stuff.

The whole thing about kids is they *do* need . . . grown-ups! And if you—if you don't have a couple of good grown-ups on your side, you cannot—you could go down! Or if you don't have ones that can *deal* with the system. You need grown-ups who are allies. You just can't make it—kids can't. You know, 'cause you look at a lotta kids who go "But *for* . . . I would be in prison." And a lot of that is around a teacher or somebody who saved 'em. Somebody who just—who reached out to them, and went like, "Come on, you can do this," you know? "This is gonna be okay. But you gotta stop acting like this. You can't run from the cops, 'cause if you run from the cops they chase you."

And one of the things we looked at was how *overmedicated* foster children are. The biggest expense in Medicaid in this county—in this state [of California], is for psychotropic drugs for foster children! All they do is jack these kids up on medicine. We're using drugs to control children. 'Mean, you look at yourself and you go, what kind of people do that.

Y'know what I mean, *c'mon*, these are children, y'know?

And I mean, it's like, did you see that—that video of the fourteen-year-old girl in Texas?

(*Behind her, an actual cell phone video from June 5, 2015, of a fourteen-year-old black girl in a bathing suit being thrown to the ground by a white police officer in Texas. From the video: the sound of teenagers screaming. The girl on the ground cries out: "I want my*

mama. I want my mama. Oh God!" The police officer: "Get down! On your face!")

She's crying for her *mommy.* "Mama, Mama, I want my mama." And she's in a *bathing* suit! Like what kind of <u>threat</u> is this? Who—who does that to a fourteen-year-old?

I think judges . . . I—I think we've gone to sleep on the job, I really do. US law is justice by strangers, y'know, and that's how it—you keep yourself separate. You *do* that and I just don't believe in it! When they had problems with each other, we resolved it in the village. With—sometimes we used elders to help us. If we really needed to. But we did not go to strangers. When I was on the bench in San Francisco, my—the way I made it work for me was to use the values that I'm familiar with, which meant that I treated the people who appeared in front of me as if they were my family. Y'know, I don't think . . . And I don't really feel like I *judge,* I *help* . . . people meet responsibilities.

To *me* the problem is that nobody learned that justice is what—what the law is about. Yes, you need rules—every society needs rules—but the whole thing about having a law or having a process or having courts was to ensure fairness and right behavior and justice! It's not about that anymore. It's about money. It's about . . . you know, whoever has the power to . . .

I think the country's broken. I really do.

(*The musician exits the stage.*)

EDUCATION AND SURVIVAL

LETICIA DE SANTIAGO

PARENT
STOCKTON, CALIFORNIA

"The Geese"

"The Geese"

(*An elegant, dignified woman in her fifties. Salvadoran accent. Sitting in a conference room at Fathers & Families—a nonprofit dedicated to helping recently released inmates transition back into the community, offers help finding jobs, etc. She volunteers here regularly. Swivel office chair. Musician is onstage. He sometimes interacts with the actor.*)

But it's—I think it's the way . . . you raise your kids. What they see around the family. I never heard too much about drugs at that time, but it was more about baggy pants and you start being in gangs? That's what I was worried. (*Listens to a question.*)

I don't see *nothing* in the pants; what I see is *butts* all the time. You can see the *underwear*! I don't have the *slightest* idea why the kids do it. And I—I don't think I would let my kids do it. I wouldn't let them. No! I woulda ripped every single pants. Knowing myself I would have done it!

One of the parents told me that [my kids] used to go to their homes? And change. Then I became very good friends with their parents. And we all used to communicate. And I think that was the key. One of the mothers [is] the one who told me [that my kids were wearing baggy pants]. And *that's* when I went to the school and say—I say, "What are you doing with those pants?" Or "How are you doing to those pants?" They say, "Oh, Mom, these are my friends." Say, "Come on, don't make me embarrassing here at school." Say, "Okay, we gonna talk when we get home." And we talking, I tell him, I say, "Okay, I'm gonna meet you halfway. Not that baggy. A little bit loose. But I don't want you to be going to nobody's house and change."

I feel that I was a very strict mother. And I was very involved in their school. And their—anything that it was involving my kids, I was very involved. Very involved.

At nighttime, I used to go and smell them, and—yes. To see if they were not smoking or drinking. Oh, yes. I did so many things to keep my kids outta trouble. And thanks to the Lord, I think I did a good job.

We moved to Vallejo, and from Vallejo, that's when I started having problems. 'Cause they were in that age, at thirteen, fourteen years old? That—that the um—the . . . the school [was] calling me, that they didn't come to school. And that's when I used to communicate with the teachers all the time. *All* the time. At least once a week. I used to call. And they knew. They knew that Mommy was gonna come.

Uh, with my daughter? Gah, was worse with her. My concern was for my daughter not to become pregnant. She was very beautiful, yeah. What I did is that I start take her to model—modeling? Modeling. Yeah. From there I used to—uh, she compete from San Joaquin. Miss San Joaquin here? She didn't win, but that open the doors for . . . She went to uh Miami, Cancún. She, uh, won in Cancún? Miss Cancún? And—and the reason why I did that was the requirement was to be in school. And not to be pregnant, not to have kids.

I used to even—we were having some goose? Goose? I think it's what you call goose, they're worse than dogs? The kids used to, you know, they used to get up at nighttime? Take the cars out?

The goose? The goose? The geese? The geese? The goose or the geese? Geese, yes.

The *dog*—they knew the dogs, they didn't bark or anything, but the *geese*? Oh *no*! That's when I find out they were taking the car, too. And you could hear—the geese, they don't stop. When they see a stranger, they go, "*Voo, voo-voo, voo.*" And one time I woke up. I say, "Wow, what is that noise?' And heard the garage door. And I came downstairs, and . . . I call the police on my own kid. And his friend was begging me and, "Mrs. De Santiago. Please don't—don't—don't—don't call my parents. Don't call the police." I say, "I have to do it."

It was a gift, that someone gave me? And I did not know that they were that [good]—they worse than dogs. They are *so* good. They died. But I, uh—they did so good on me that when—how do you say, when you stuff it? [They did so good on me, that when they died] I sent for them to be stuffed. And I have them in my house. And they know, my kids know. They say, "This is Rosita and this is Frankie." They know, because they have memories.

I had to move from Vallejo. I say, "I have to move from here." 'Cause I—I didn't want none of my kids to go to jail. You know, you start seeing a lot of things, in the news, I don't want none of my kids . . . none of *my* family. Who wants that? *Nobody.*

TONY EADY

STUDENT CONCERNS SPECIALIST, NORTH CHARLESTON HIGH SCHOOL
NORTH CHARLESTON, SOUTH CAROLINA

"All Because of Your Mouth"

"All Because of Your Mouth"

(*African American. In his fifties. Mild South Carolina accent. With a walkie-talkie, which is on. ID on a lanyard. Conference room at the school, or hallway or cafeteria. Deep, resonant voice.*)

These kids are very, very defiant. Very defiant. I am a student concerns specialist here at North Charleston High School in Charleston, South Carolina. I am the eyes and ears of the campus for the principal.

I used to work in a penitentiary, and I used to work a—in Florida. Maximum security penitentiary. (*He chuckles.*) I had the privilege of meeting Ted Bundy—Theodore Bundy—when he was down there.

I often tell some of my colleagues that it is similar. [The kids] just get to go home. But the control piece is: never let the kids [in the school] or the inmates [in a prison] get you out of your character. You have to be ready. You have to *prepare* yourself. When you come into these places. When you come into these places because (*slight pause*) the inmates or the students have their own agenda. This job can cause you to step out of [your] character. It means you can get unprofessional sometimes. You know, because the kids challenge you. *Every* day. So you gotta be ready.

I do what they—we call ISS here. And that's in-school suspension. I do that in the mornings, uh, every other week. And, um, when I get a group of [kids] in there, I talk to them about— 'Cause I tell the kids, "You guys comin' into ISS here . . ." And then we have we call Twilight also—that's worse than ISS. That's on the third floor. So I *tell* the kids, "This is just a rehearsal! When you—

when you always comin' into ISS, that means you can't deal with the public, the society in school. So they always send you here!"

I say, "That's a rehearsal! When you out in society, if—if you can't deal with authority figures and people tellin' you what to do, they gonna—to send you to jail." This is—I call it school jail. (*As one of the kids:*) "I'm not in no school jail!" (*As himself:*) "Yes, you are. 'Cause you incarcerated here for this hour. You can't *leave*. And then if you act up in here, then they send you to Twilight." And I call that "penitentiary." That's *worse* than ISS 'cause you in there all day, every day. For months. So I say, "If you don't learn how to deal with authority figures, when you finish high school or drop out or quit or *whatever* . . . it's gonna—same thing's gonna happen in the real world. This is just a rehearsal!"

I tell the kids this—when you get on that bus. You get sentenced. You get on that bus and you are heading to one of these institutions. You have to *change*. You can't be the same person that you [were when you] walked into the courtroom. You have to be— You have to change. You can't be the same person because they are not normal people back there. Everybody is trying to get after you, or get over on you or— (*Abrupt stop, brief pause.*) It's different. It's just different. You have to step out of your character. There's animals back there. That's a different world. People get raped, people get beat on, people get murdered people get stabbed, there's nowhere to run nowhere to hide. This is *real*. And they buildin' a lot of 'em. They buildin' more of those than they buildin' schools. So I tell 'em yeah, it's real.

And I heard a police officer, one of my good friends, say that most people get incarcerated because of their mouth. They— What they *say*, when they approached by authority figures, you know. "Get out the car." "Why do I have to get out the car for?"

When they do get out the car, and questioning. This is some of the things that they say, so. "Why you stopping me?" "Wh— what's up, man?" And the officer goes from that to, "Get out of the car." Now, "Wh—what do you want me to get out of the car for?" Then they call for backup. And *more* coming.

[I been here] twenty-three years. Sometimes I ask God, "Why—why am I still here?" It's a constant fight, every day, with the kids and disrespect, and just trying to get them to do the right thing; it's just wearing on me so. I've stood between kids and the principal, Mr. Grimm, and I could see when it's going a wrong way, and I gotta intercept.

And let me give you an example: Well, a—a kid got put outta his class for a cell phone. Kids? Cell phones? They would rather go to jail then give up their cell phones! And I'm standin' outside with the kid, and Mr. Grimm walks up, 'cause he hears the call. "What's the problem?" "Well, Mr. Grimm, he's . . . refused to give the cell phone out, but I—I have it now." And then the kid'll say, "Yeah, you might have it *now*, but I'm gonna get my phone back!" Mr. Grimm says, "Excuse me?" (*As the student:*) "You heard what I s—" And I try to intercept. Cause I see: now you challenging the authority figure—the bigger top-authority figure. I know where it's *going*! Because Mr. Grimm's not gonna let him talk to him like that. So he's gonna respond with something like, "Oh, well I'mma *get* your phone and I'mma *keep* your phone." Then [the kid] may say something like, "No!" Probably reach for the phone, or step for the phone, "Gimme my phone!" And they try to get it.

And that went from: you just giving up your phone; you get-ting it back next period. Now you not getting you phone. And you bein' arrested. Being suspended. Maybe up for expulsion. *All* because of your mouth.

[These kids] *really* don't *care.* They don't have respect for—for nobody. And then, society tells you, "You *can't* touch 'em. You *can't* grab them." And the *kids* know that. So, I mean, they don't stop! These kids just get . . . more *power* added to them.

[Then people don't want police officers in the schools.] A police officer's gonna take control of the situation! So *why* put them in school if you don't want them take control of the situation? I *need* police officers in the school. I *need* for me, I *need* a police officer to take control. I need a kid to see that there is an authority in a *school*! He's my—*our* last line of defense.

THE SHAKARA STORY

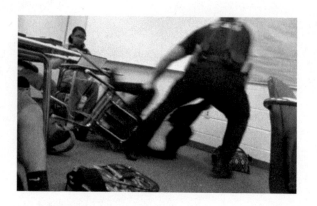

A cell phone video of Shakara, a student at Spring Valley High School, being thrown across the room by school resource officer Deputy Ben Fields on October 26, 2015.

The actor sits in front of a screen. Wearing a hoodie that could pass either in the South Bronx or on Madison Avenue, in that hip-hop fashion way. The hoodie is worn for both Amanda Ripley and Niya Kenny. Next to the chair, a water bottle.

[Slide]

AMANDA RIPLEY

JOURNALIST
WASHINGTON, DC

"The Shakara Story"

"The Shakara Story"

(*Amanda is a very fit woman in her early forties. She plays soccer. You can tell she's an athlete because of the efficiency of her movements and her posture. She has a very friendly demeanor. She is a journalist and has a bit of an intrepid air about her. An obvious sense of humor. Wearing sandals. The interview was done during the summertime in Washington, DC.*)

Niya Kenny. Who was the oldest girl in the class. She was sitting there in this Algebra 1 class that she'd failed as a freshman and needed to pass to graduate. And she was doing well in that class actually! So she's [an] eighteen-year-old African American girl, and she—she had a good rapport with the teacher, she had an A average, and she's working on a—each of them working on their laptops. Uh, on . . . *math* problems.

And [Niya] sees the teacher whisper something. She sees the whisp—the teacher, Mr. Long, who's a veteran math teacher, white man, whisper something to one of the other kids in the class. A girl. Who doesn't—she doesn't—Niya doesn't know her name, but she doesn't talk much, she's new to the class, this girl. Shakara. As it turns out. And then Niya sees Mr. Long go back to his desk and pick up the phone and call for someone to escort someone outta the classroom.

And Niya looks at Shakara and she says (*acting this out*), "You?" Like, "Is this for you?" Like, she mouths. And Shakara nods, and she [Niya] thought that was strange, 'cause . . . she hadn't seen . . . I guess apparently, you know, Shakara had taken out her phone. We still don't know exactly why or what happened, but she didn't . . . Either she wouldn't put it away or she wouldn't give it up. I think it was that she wouldn't give up her phone. *To* the teacher. Sometimes, at that school, if you take out your phone, they'll take it for the day. It's pretty routine policy.

So, for whatever reason, that we still don't know, Shakara got in trouble with this teacher. And um he called the assistant principal, Mr. Webb, who came, and according to Niya, uh, he said [to Shakara], "Come with me." Or something to that effect. And Shakara declined to come. And then, according to Niya, he said something to the effect of "I ain't got time to play with y'all today." And he turned around and he left.

And Niya saw him return. (*As if answering a question.*) Black man. And he came back with . . . uh . . . Deputy Fields. Who's sort of a large, hulking, uhh, white, police officer. Who also is uh—football coach at the school. And when Niya saw him, she says—she said to the boy sitting next to her, "Take out your phone." So she took her phone out, too, because she had a feeling, she heard stories about this guy—she had a feeling he might do something, you know . . . *worthy* (*an ironic half laugh*) . . . of being videotaped . . . uhh and so.

Well you know what's on the video. When [Deputy Fields] uh, you know, asked [Shakara] to leave. And [Shakara] wouldn't leave with him. And he removed her laptop to the other desk. And he tried to extract [Shakara] from the chair . . . um . . . um . . . rather violently. . . . And then he did eventually extract her from the chair. And Niya filmed this and was getting more and more distraught.

NIYA KENNY

FORMER STUDENT, SPRING VALLEY HIGH SCHOOL
COLUMBIA, SOUTH CAROLINA

"The Shakara Story"

"The Shakara Story"

(*Niya was eighteen at the time of the first interview. Calm, self-possessed, open. Wearing simple clothing. There were two interviews. One took place in a small conference room at a public library in Columbia, South Carolina. The other took place in a rehearsal hall in New York City nine months later. She was more glamorous at that time, having moved to New York.*)

He's—he's like, wrestling, trying to get her arms behind her back at this time. On the floor. And they were wrestling for, like, a minute, too. It took Deputy Bradley to come in and get her in handcuffs.

That's what I was thinking, too! This man is, like, three hundred pounds, body builder, and you couldn't get her . . . I don't know. She was like, kinda—her arms were may—in some kind of way. Maybe he thought, you know, "I would break her arm if I just go like this." (*She gestures.*) So maybe he wasn't trying to do that. But I—I don't—I really don't know what was going through his head, her head, or anything. I know he couldn't get her in those handcuffs. That's all.

I was like, "*Is nobody gonna help her?*" I'm like: "*Somebody record this! Put it on Snapchat!*" And then I'm askin' Mr. Webb and Mr. Long, I'm just like: "*Look,*" like, what I— "*Nobody's gonna help her?*" I turn to Mr. Long, I'm just like: "*You did this! You didn't even have to call the administrator!*" I was just . . . (*Breathes out, long and heavy.*)

AMANDA RIPLEY: And then she says, "What the *fuck*! What the *fuck*!" And then the teacher—the assistant principal says, "Niya . . . Niya . . ." and tries to—to calm her down. And she won't *be* calmed down, and then the cop turns to her and says—and—and says—and—and says something, we don't know what, but according to [Niya], something like, "You got so much to say? 'Cause you're coming next."

And then he [Deputy Fields] comes back, after he takes Shakara, and he comes back. He . . . um . . . Niya at that point becomes passive, because she realizes he's not joking, and she stands up and puts her hands behind her back and he handcuffs her and—and then he takes [Niya] to *another* room, where Shakara is.

Shakara's kind of leaning down, she's still handcuffed. She's got her braids falling in her face. And he flips the braids out of Shakara's face? And he says to her, according to Niya, "Did you take your meds today?" And this is the *one* thing Shakara says. She finally says something. She says: "Yes. Did *you*?"

Which I thought was great! That was great, that was a great teenage response right there. And uh . . . just perfect.

And then he leaves again. And then Shakara's apparently released into the care of a guardian. She's in foster care. I don't know which guardian.

And then Niya Kenny is eighteen, so she's considered an adult. So she's sittin' there waiting. Still handcuffed. And she hears over Fields's walkie-talkie that the uh the transport is here. And she starts crying. 'Cause she knows that's for her and he's not joking. Like she keeps thinking, "*Maybe* he's gonna release me. Maybe it's just to scare me." And she goes outside, and there's a paddy wagon—police paddy wagon, right? They drive Niya to the detention center. It was an adult jail.

NIYA KENNY: The whole time I was thinking about, "I'm embarrassing my mom. My mom's gonna be mad. She's gonna kill me." Like, "Mom, Mom, Mom." That's the only person I'm thinking about. I was like, "Oh God, I'm gonna get outta this jail and she's gonna beat me right in the yard."

But everybody in the jail was like normal people to me. Everybody was nice, y'know. When they saw the video on the TV news, they was like, "Whaaa . . ." Everybody. Everybody was like, "Whaaaaa . . . He threw that little girl like that? And you was in there? Oh, *girl* you goin' *home*, you goin' *home*."

And then when I saw [the video] on the news, when I saw the video, I was like, "I know she saw it!" The first thing that—that, uh, went through my mind was like, "My mom saw it! I know she did! I'm not in trouble anymore! I'm not in trouble!" So I call my mom, and she was like, "Niya, you don't even know. The news is out here. They wanna interview you. *Good Morning America* is coming to the house tonight—"

I don't know. I don't know what it is. It's just somethin' inside of me, that I don't know, makes me snap, when I see people bein' mistreated, I guess. I'm talking about elementary school, I *never* held my tongue. One time in third grade, one of my friends was bein' bad in class in third grade. And my teacher was, um . . . was (*whispering*) a *white* lady. You know, and I knew about racism, because my dad had always taught his kids, like, since we were in kindergarten, like, always raised us to know about racism, like, "Know your history." So one time she grabbed this boy—like, picked him up by his *cheek* out of the chair. And I just lost it. I lost it! Lost it in the classroom. I was like, "You are not his mom! You can't touch him like that! That is—that's not your job! Your job is to teach us! You do not pick a student up by his cheek out of the chair!" Like, yeah. I was really mad. And um . . . she wrote me up for bein' disrespectful and um belligerent. And so that was my first after-school detention. Yeah. So that's why—that's why I feel like I was born, y'know, with this. Because what third grader do you know would've stood up for, you know, her friend after the teacher pinch his cheek?

(*She listens to a question.*)

Shakara? We—we didn't really—on—we—we didn't really talk. Like, throughout this whole year. We—we talked, but not like . . . maybe people expected us to? I don't know? Like, talk every single day, like, "We're close friends now." We're—we're still just as distant as we were before I stood up for her. And initially, I was like, "Is this girl, like, ungrateful?" Like, "I literally sat in jail for a day for standing up for you." But . . . at the same time, you know, I was also—not at the same time, 'cause that was like me initially thinking. But after that, thinking more on it, I just figured it was because—I don't know, like, maybe she wanted to be alone? Maybe . . . I knew that she didn't wanna always talk about, you know, the incident, and so when I did reach out to her, it was never talking about that. It was like, "How are you doing? Do you need anything?" You know, like, "If"—always telling her—"if you need anything, I'm here." But she's never reached out to me for anything. (*She listens to a question.*) She's actually in a home right now. Like, one of those group homes. I don't know how she ended up there.

I knew when they told my mom, when the school called her, they were gonna say, "Niya got in something that didn't involve her." And that's exactly what they did. So I knew her mind-set was gonna be, "Oh, Niya. Why didn't you be quiet?"

You know, because that's the response I got in third grade. You know, and "Mind your business, it didn't have nothin' to do with you." And I'm, "But she picked this boy up by his cheek!" You know?

And then, *they're* telling me, "Mind your business, this didn't have nothing to do with you." "But he just threw a whole girl across the classroom!" How can you mind your business? Like, that's somethin' you need to *make* your business.

ACT TWO

A CANDLE IN THE VILLAGE

SARI MUHONEN

TEACHER AND TEACHER EDUCATOR
UNIVERSITY OF HELSINKI TEACHER TRAINING SCHOOL
HELSINKI, FINLAND

"Handcuffs"

"Handcuffs"

(*Summertime in Helsinki. Elementary school classroom. Bright graphics on bulletin boards. Sunshine. Blond, very friendly. On her knees, on a student's chair, leaning over a student's desk, holding a cellphone, studying the same video of the incident at Spring Valley High School that ended Act One. The video is projected on a screen behind her so that we see what she is watching. She is amazed and shocked at what she sees. Making faces, covering her eyes, then peeking out at the video again. A series of phonetic sounds in response to the horror of what she sees.*)

(*Making faces, covering her eyes.*) Ooohf. Slaptofluh Tzuh No Tzuh Ohhh! Tsieh. That's— (*Looking out.*) Well, I have never seen like this in Finland. Never. Nowhere. So I think this is quite— quite eye-opening, I would say.

Where this was? Spring Valley High [South Carolina]. (*Pause.*) So you are—you are kind of working on this issue? That's very bad. I should come to see it because I haven't— Well, something went terribly wrong, I would say.

It was girl? (*Listens.*) Because she was . . . ? (*Listens.*) What is *handcuffed*? (*Listens, shocked.*) Ahh? (*High-pitched sound.*) Noooooo. That's—that's quite amazing. But I have to say that I haven't been—because it may be that we are such a small country that maybe our problems are not—I don't know. Why would they put them— Have you seen the situation? That's really strange. That sounds quite a—quite amazing, I would say. So, I—I—I can't find a situation that—that I would need handcuffs. But! But! I have nee—but I—I have to say, I have needed a help of a colleague. But I have need a help of a colleague. Yes. Yes. So, so, uh,

I have had a very difficult person that—that was a very aggressive at—at the classroom so and—and towards each other and—
and he—he—he didn't—didn't—so, of course there have to be
some—I hope so. But still it looks—seems, I think, quite amazing
that someone would need to have handcuffs.

But anyway it was—it was, uh, it was a fighting situation. He—
he was, um, he was aggressive and very, ehm—ehm explodedly
aggressive. And—and doing mit—other—and couldn't—couldn't
make it down. (*Gesturing to show how she tried to control the
child.*) So although I do it like this way? And doing like this for
me also. And then I had the—take like this and say, "Go and—
and find another person here." And I wouldn't have—have, uh,
needed handcuffs either. Of course, um, it's difficult if you have—
have—have persons that are aggressive. But still—still I—I don't
think on handcuffs also. Really.

Okay. So you performing me? And you could do it? (*Facial
expression.*) Okay. Well, uh, I'm Sari Muhonen, and I'm a teacher,
um, and a teacher educator. And I teach at the University of Helsinki Viikki Teacher Training School, where I teach as, uh, in primary classroom, currently at fifth grade. And also I teach a lot
of music and conduct the choir. And, um, also part of my—my
thing is um doing research on, on developing practices in our
school. Scientific research.

Discipline [here] works, ahm, aaaahm (*higher note*) . . . Well,
there is no one—one way, of course. It always depends on the
situation. So there is no recipe for that. But of course I think,
um, it—whenever possible—it's the—it's the most important
thing is—is when you have the—the classroom for the first time
that you really concentrate: "I see you. And you are very welcome here." So I think I try to—try to formulate the situation so
that they—it would be preventative. But of course that does not

always . . . help? So (*laugh*), but there are (*laugh*), there are many. (*Laugh, laugh.*) Yes. But—but—I think that is one of the issues so that they are not just a mass coming in and going out. Because I'm a classroom teacher. This is *my* class. And this is *our* class. And I try to build very strong relationship.

I have some Finnish colleagues who have been writing about this, at least in Finnish, but I know there are En-English: "pedagogical love." So I know of—I don't know if I would say that I *love* the children in my classroom. But I care of them very much. And, "I care of you. And why do you *act* like this?" (*Slight pause.*) And—and I try to talk with them. And sometimes I go and touch them. And sometimes it helps, and sometimes it does not. And then you have to be—harder.

Yeah. Yeah. Yes. Yes. Yeah. Yeah. And of course—of course I-I-I shouldn't also give you too good impression of Finland also. So of course we have bad-behaving persons here also. And if somebody tries even a little, I can look and: "<u>Whattt?</u> (*Beat.*) Did you say?" And they understand it. Yes! I can do that! Yes! I can do that! But I know that in the upper grades also in Finland there are bad-behaving persons who maybe to—to rebellion. Perhaps saying that "I'm not doing that." But police officers I don't think is needed anywhere. I have never heard. No. No. We are adults. (*Sudden conclusive stop. Listens.*)

It has been said that, um, [in Finland] the teacher was always—was a candle in the—a candle in the village. So in the former times also. (*Beat.*) And it's also research-based. So having a kind of developing nature in your—your career, I think that also goes perhaps to the issue of narration. (*Slight pause.*)

Finland is a—such a small country. And we—we have quite a— We have not had so long for— We are quite homogeneous country for so long. (*Listens.*)

[Immigration?] Yes, there are some schools I think in eastern Helsinki that . . .

For instance, this school was for—in former times in very (*gestures each time there is a quotation mark*) "good" area. Very "old" area. Very "Finnish" area. And when we moved here in Viikki, there is also many Somalian children. And many—many Russian children. And many uh Latvia children. Seventy percent of the children are already foreign-based. And it—it's really—it's really um something that maybe is becoming more and more to—to think about. That is something that has been discussed here more and more in Finland. That we are going to be more diverse country. And it's quite new issue for us. And—and it was—it was a very new situation for us. That was very uhm very uhm kind of finding new ways. (*Pause.*)

You are talking about race and racial issues. Maybe our eyes are not so open to these issues. (*Pause.*) Because you never know— Because there may be some, I dunno, problems if some people in—in Finland— I haven't—have never encountered this— But I could think that in US might be somewhere that they are taking some kind of drug or something so that they are—I dunno— aggressive. Or—I dunno. Tell me about it.

[Slide]

DENISE DODSON

INMATE, MARYLAND CORRECTIONAL INSTITUTION FOR WOMEN
STUDENT, GOUCHER PRISON EDUCATION PARTNERSHIP
JESSUP, MARYLAND

"That, *That* Was It and That Was *All*"

"That, *That* Was It and That Was *All*"

(*A loud prison sound. A gate slamming. Dodson is soft-spoken, poised. Sitting in a chair with a legal pad, a pen, and reading glasses on her lap. Wears a T-shirt, blue cotton prison pants. She wears winter-style hiking boots, though it's the middle of summer. Thoughtful, humble, but self-possessed, apparent wisdom. Sitting very still, no superfluous movements. At some point an announcement will blast over the PA system, interrupting the monologue momentarily.*)

And now I'm in college [here at the Maryland Correctional Institution] and I see where I've missed out on a *lot*. A lotta information, a lot of important information that . . . would've helped me make better decisions. As far as, the—uhhm . . . my baby's father? The people that I chose to, to actually be with, uhhm, and planned to spend my life with? I kinda gravitated to my environment versus reaching out *past* the environment, and I started believing that *that* was it and that was *all*. Uhhm. And the only thing that was required *of* me was *for* me. And that was basically . . . to feed my*self*. And the baby that I was carrying in it.

Everything was *me*, it was never like—the next-door neighbor could be going through the same thing. If I was educated in, to that degree, then I would've made better decisions. Uhhm . . . I guess I can say that I just wasn't connecting to everything, because I wasn't given enough information to know that we all are connected somehow. To every living, breathing thing. And I didn't *get* that.

But this experience has showed me how connected I really am to the person next door, down the street or whatever.

Uhhm, how important it is to come together and ... I've learned how the government work. Like, I didn't— I never understood that, what was the governor for, or what, you know, was the mayor for. I don't get it, I don't understand, I understand that they are important people, but to what degree of importance, what are they there for? And I never really got that in my history classes. So to get that, now, as a grown woman, is like, whoa.

(*Listens to a question.*)

Finding out what this world is really all about, how it revolves, what's expected of you as a citizen? Basically to work together? In a unit? To pave the way for those who are coming *behind* us. Uhhm, to make better living arrangements for everybody as a whole? Because of, I mean at the end of the day, it's about living. And it's about living *properly*. And it's about educating others and, uh, rearing your children properly. So that *they* can be productive and ... and not be barbaric, basically!

(*Listens to a question.*) I had six children, now I have five, one has passed away since I been here? The oldest being thirty-four and the youngest is twenty-one. I've been here for twenty-three years. Had my last child at the Baltimore City Detention Center.

(*Crying, but discreetly.*) Well, my ... boyfriend—former boyfriend, 'cause we weren't together anymore. Shot and killed the guy who tried to rape me.

(*Listens to a question.*)

They didn't—call it accomplice though, I have the same charge as he has.

(*Listens to a question.*)

First-degree murder.

(*Listens to a question, struggles to stay composed, cries quietly.*)

When you're talking about somebody's life, whether it was

(*crying*) whether it was in your control or not . . . somebody's life has been taken. So, I do think it's fair.

I think that had I had a better education, had—I would have made better decisions. I would have been more upright, so to speak. Because when I didn't have that education, I always felt less than. You know, my self-esteem wasn't the way it shouldn't have been. Had I been educated to know that, you know, I *am* somebody, I *am* a good person uhhm . . .

(*Listens to a question.*)

I just made parole. But the paperwork has to go to the governor first and he has to approve it first.

And so now that I've been raising dogs [here while I'm incarcerated] and training them to go and help people who have disabilities like—like, that's my purpose. I think it's my way of expressing love towards people who really *need*—who really need something or someone. There's a lot of people who're, like, alone, or whatever. So . . . I get a chance to express it through the dogs that I train.

(*Listens to a question.*)

I definitely trust them to carry that love. I mean they do so well here. They—very loyal and loving and—but uhhm, yeah. They're amazing.

There are times when you, when . . . you may be going through something, and people will be like, so into themselves and what they doing. I'm not saying that they're . . . just ignoring you totally, like they don't *care*? But they're not gonna stop. And give you a hug or . . . bring you up outta that emotion. They just don't do that. They'll be like, "*Oh you be ahyight!*" With a dog, it's like, it's so different. She'll jump on me, roll around on the floor, make me play with her, and then I'm like, "Okay." Get myself together, and think about how I'll move through this.

(*Listens to a question.*)

Labrador retrievers, golden retrievers, and right now I have a standard . . . labradoodle.

[How do I feel about talking to you today?] (*Softly.*) The more I talk, the better I'll get. That's how I feel. (*Louder.*) I said the more I talk, the better I'll get, that's how I feel. Because a lot of times you don't . . . it's good to hear yourself, 'cause then then you're like, thinking things through and you—you're finding out more and more about yourself, like, as I sit here, I'm finding more and more out about myself. And how connected education and survival are in me as a person. Y'know, and still have more room to grow.

[Is there anything we talked about today that I haven't thought about in a long time?] Mmm—yeah, I didn't think about school [for a long time now till today] like, elementary school, and how much I wasn't getting that attention that I needed through the teachers. I think if I had gotten that attention, I could have moved *forward* and not stayed stagnated in that, "I'm not sure if I'm doing, I'm accurate, like I'm doing the right thing." Yeah. I mean, because if you're *wrong* about something, and you have a wrong *answer*, and there's no one there to say, "Well, this is wrong and this is why," then you stay right there. That's where you stay at. So . . .

Well, if I didn't correct [the dogs], then they would be . . . yeah, they would just do anything, they'd do whatever they want. They wouldn't have no . . . boundaries. But they do. Because they're being taught. Constant. All day, every day . . . it's teaching them, and praising them, and letting them know that they're doing the right thing. And . . . we get really good results, like . . . out of a hundred dogs, eighty-nine of those dogs are gonna make it.

And I think if the teachers were more . . . involved, with the schoolwork and the children *as people*, as the little people that they really are, I think that they would progress better. Think that they would be better . . . people.

Oh! If they don't see them as little people, they—they're just seeing them as . . . They have to see 'em as people. They have to see them as the future. They have to see them as people who are gonna go out and be their next-door neighbors. So they have to see them as people and teach them all that they can, while they can. 'Cause they're . . . at that stage where they absorb everything. And if they not absorbing all the right things, then . . . yeah. That's . . . barbaric.

[Slide]

Ms. Dodson was released from prison in 2018.

TRAUMA

[Slide]

DR. VICTOR CARRION, MD

PSYCHIATRIST
DIRECTOR, STANFORD EARLY LIFE STRESS RESEARCH PROGRAM
DEPARTMENT OF PSYCHIATRY, STANFORD UNIVERSITY SCHOOL OF MEDICINE
STANFORD, CALIFORNIA

"DNA"

"DNA"

(Elegant, Puerto Rican–born man. Fine black loafers. Seated in a modern, well-appointed office. Accent slides in and out of standard American and one influenced by the Spanish language. Very careful speech, thoughtful, seemingly very aware of the consequences of what he says. Gentle manner. Musician comes onstage.)

I became interested in brain development and the effect of stress on the development of the brain. I am getting notes from teachers saying, "This child has ADHD. Please place on Ritalin." And I'm like, "Wow. The diagnosis has been made. There is a treatment plan. Am I needed for anything?" And in fact, when some of these children had an in-depth clinical evaluation, they did not have attention deficit hyperactivity disorder. But they had a long history of adversity.

And many of them had a history, not of only stress, but of traumatic stress.

[It's] a type of stress that really impacts your functional, uh . . . it—it impairs your function. So it impairs your function academically, it impairs your function socially, and it impairs how you feel—you feel distressed. And this is how these children were feeling.

(Listens to a question.)

Historical trauma exists, not only in history. It exists in our daily life. And I think as a society, we sometimes experience symptoms of post-traumatic stress disorder. Specifically avoidance. Which is a very bad symptom. Not wanting to talk about it or not thinking about it. Or not addressing it? And . . . what happens when that avoidance is there . . . the impact of the trauma permeates, it continues. But the way that it also happens is that, it goes from generation to generation. Because I see many children, and now I see many adults, that may not have the trauma experiences in their lives. They have learned that as a response, from caretakers.

They model it.

Now, some individuals think that this actually may be passed also epigenetically. Where there may be some changes in coding of—of DNA. Where—where you actually alter your DNA, and then what you're passing is an altered DNA.

(*Listens to a question.*)

Slavery? (*Considers this very carefully. Begins next sentence tentatively, then picks up speed.*) The social factors that are—surround the issue of of slavery and the history of slavery are enough that they don't need any DNA change. (*Quick stop.*) Because in the way in which they have resulted in many populations of African Americans living in a state of poverty where it's very hard for them to escape from. It's a way of maintaining that enslavement. And of course, it's not only in African Americans. But I think many communities that are African American have gone from a history of slavery to another form of slavery, y'know, through poverty.

(*Musician exits.*)

[Slide]

STEVEN CAMPOS

FORMER INMATE
DISHWASHER, DISNEY HALL
LOS ANGELES, CALIFORNIA

"Microwave"

"Microwave"

(Sitting in a straightbacked chair by a window in a loft in down-town LA. Not his loft, just the place where the interview took place. Salvadoran. In his early twenties. White "wifebeater" T-shirt, black chinos, wide belt, tennis shoes. Sitting completely straight, hands folded. Small of stature. Not a lot of movement. Looking at inter-viewer/audience very directly. Often stops at the end of a thought, pausing for the impact but with no expression on his face. Wide smile sometimes, even when the content is dark. Obviously very intelligent. He sounds almost like a '50s beat poet. His demeanor changes toward the end, when he becomes effusively upset.)

Trauma, shit, anybody can— Anything that a freaking . . . They say they went to school for all that bullshit and all that shit. No. Hell no. You can fake their asses like a lot. Shit, I seen a motha-fucker fake trauma, to the max— *(Sudden stop.)*
   (Listens to a question.)
   Ummm he was acting like he was traumatized by what he did, and everything he got: they had to comfort him like a little baby. Hell yeah! He confused them. You can trick a therapist into giv-ing you meds, and he would do it, and he really would fall for it. You can trick therapists! They're supposed to know when you are telling them a lie and they wouldn't even know. I tricked 'em, told him I couldn't go to sleep, and he gave me sleeping meds? I seen other kids just say stupid shit, and they got meds, just to get meds, tweaking meds . . .
   Some motherfuckers gangbang and all that shit? NO! You PUT yourself in that position. It's like, I put MYself in that situa-

tion. Yeah. Shit, we all . . . you knew what you were doing before you . . . shit, if you didn't, you wouldn't have got yourself in it! Or else you were too damn retarded.

(*Listens to a question.*)

Historical trauma? That's bullshit! That's bullshit! I'm Salvadoran. <u>Hell</u> no. They ain't mess half my people up. Blacks, they don't . . . *Dude. Man.* Most of blacks who are incarcerated n'even *care* about slavery. They just move on like another part of their . . . They be like, "It ain't *my* time. I wuzzin' there, so what do I care about it?" Yeah, a lot of it is bullshit. Only to *some*—yeah, they care about it. Only to ones that really care about the *real* past—o' the black, like *activists*, *they* really care about it. But the blacks, no, *hell* no.

They just gotta change 'em internally. You want to change, you just going to have to do it by yourself, or—and get help. People will help you but mainly, you gonna have to do by yourself, like I'm doing. (*Burp.*) As soon as I came out, gotta job.

(*Listens to a question.*)

Dishwasher at Disney Hall. Downtown LA. Got my substance abuse. Stayin' away from the homies. Stop drinking and smoking. Trying to get my mind right, get back on track. Get enrolled in college.

(*Listens to a question.*)

I'mma go into nursing. I was always fascinated about bein' around open wounds. Blood don't creep me out, and so you know, perfect job for me. I signed up for Los Angeles City College. I just got in yesterday, they emailed me that I got accepted.

(*Listens to a question.*)

My mother's happy that me, my brother, and all her brothers are out, 'cause we all did— They went to prison, I went to YA. . . .

It's all about what you wanna do. It's not "Aw, I can't do it, aww, my mind's too fucked up." No, it's none of that. If you want your mine *like* that, you gonna have your mine like that; if you really wanna change and do all of that shit you wanna do? Then you gon' do it.

Trauma. Motherfucking *act* like to max. *Some,* some cases that's true, and some it's not. To the sexos? Yeah, that's true, they have some fucked-up lives. Sex offenders? They have some fucked-up lives. They repeat what they did ha—what happened to them. So, yeah, I understand sexos, cause they have some fucked-up lives. Oh, yeah, a sexo put a k—a baby in a fucking (*snaps his fingers*) uh microwave and let it pop. Man, let that motherfucker pop. Now that's some fucked-up shit. (*Solid stop and pause, as if patiently waiting for that idea to land.*)

(*Listens to a question.*)

I don't know <u>what</u> the fuck happened in that motherfucker, damn! That 'fucker put a microwave and a baby and make that motherfucker *pop*! 'At's some sick <u>shit</u>. (*Solid stop.*)

You gotta be a lunatic to do some shit like that. (*Solid stop.*)

Not even the hardest *vatos* I know would do some shit like that. (*Solid stop.*)

Not even the hardest gang members I know would do some shit like that. (*Solid stop.*)

Even we'll look at you like you retarded. Why the *fuck* would you kill a *baby*? We frown upon that shit, we don't fucking do that, baby, we don't fuck an innocent, we don't we don't like doing that shit. It happens! I can't lie . . . but . . . We *frown* upon that shit. That's just like, the fuck do they got to do with it? We try to keep that shit as separate as we can. But shit happens.

(*Listens to a question.*)

I'll smoke that motherfucker. I'll kill that motherfucker. I don't stand for that shit.

(*Listens to a question.*)

Yeah, I believe in capital punishment. Hell yeah! 'Specially for sexos! 'N' muderers! Fuck it! You get caught for it, oh well, you *did*. Shit, you you dumb enough to get caught for it. You fuck! It's yo' bad.

[Slide]

STEPHANIE WILLIAMS

EMOTIONAL SUPPORT TEACHER
PHILADELPHIA, PENNSYLVANIA

"A Tree Out of the Ground"

"A Tree Out of the Ground"

(*African American woman, mid- to late-twenties. Healthy, friendly, vulnerable, emotionally available, generous. Wonderfully expressive with hands as well as voice. Hand and body movements are always connected to meaning, never random—almost like choreography. Sitting on a sofa, horizontally. Lots of pillows. Fast-talking, like a saxophone, except when thinking something through. Musician is onstage.*)

It was (*very long pause*) Huey Elementary School? I was an emotional support teacher. And itttt was . . . it was rough.

I never . . . realized . . . how bad a situation could be . . . until . . . I worked with that population.

You have *ten* of the most needy children—kids that need *food. Shelter. Clothes. Love*, like . . . an *education*. They—just—need—so—much. And you're just one person.

Like . . . In retrospect, I really did all I could. I worked myself *to* the bone. I felt hopeless. I just felt like *really* hopeless in the situation. I felt like I had a whole bunch of starving hungry people, and I had *nothing* in my hands to give them. Even though I tried to give them so much? They had seen so much of life? And so much rough stuff? They were just like, "What's school?" Like, y'know what I mean? You get seventh graders that are smoking weed, "What's school?" You get seventh graders that are outside all hours a night? Like, how am I to keep them in the classroom? Incentives. Like incentivizing them.

And I spent so much time with my heart racing. There'd be so many fights that would, like, you know, spontaneously like start to fight or s— Y'know, "Somebody looking me the wrong way!" "*Bitch*, what the fuck you looking at, *bitch*? I fuck you up, duh—duh—duh—duh!" No, no, not to me, they say it to, like, somebody else. Here goes my heart start racin'. But like the thing is, I—I mean, I don't wanna sound—I ran that classroom. I ran a tight ship. I broke *everything* up.

It's hard to—it's hard to be that strong day in and day out. It really is. Like it got a point where people were like, "*Tss!*" Like, you know, when a new kid would come in? (*In a student's voice.*) "*Tss!* Don't fuck with Miss Williams, she'll tear you up! Don't fuck with her. You better leave her alone she—she's." Whatever.

It's *hard* to—it's hard to be that strong day in—and—day—out. It really *is*. But it's, like, to go through that all day, is like—is like beeeeinggg—it's like being in jail without a gun. It's like me running a jail without a gun. That's what it was like. Running a jail. Without a gun. Everybody for themselves, but I want you to maintain order. No guns, no handcuffs, no billy clubs. I can't throw you in a closet, I can't do any of that. It's just like, I gotta keep you in order just by being me!

An IEP is an individualized education plan. And for a st—child that's in special education and which—the majority of, you know, our kids are—do have special needs, they'll have an IEP. I mean our poor kids, our black kids, our, you know—our inner-city and rural kids. The majority of our inner-city and rural kids have IEPs. But it's for anybody that has a need that stretches outside of the general ed curriculum. And for a kid that's eighteen or seventeen, you can go back from basically from when they're three for kids that have had early intervention and see the types of things that they've gone through, you know? Um and as a special educator, administrator, we have access to files and they're this big and if you go through it it's—you see these kids' stories. It's funny, when I first read IEPs, I'm like, "Oh shit. Oh, they throw desks, they do this, they do that." You get to see this person, like, in person, and they just blow your mind; they're nothing like their paperwork. But then when you see all the things that they've gone through in the paperwork, you gotta look at them and be like, "Damn!" You know? More power to you, like you're—you're still here, like. Like, when you hear these kids' stories and the things that—they've gone through, and some of it—I can relate to them.

But it's like, like everybody y'know, I had a little bit of self-esteem issue, but my mom, whenever—she—would—drop—me—off—to—school, she'd always—say, "Why do you have to work harder than everybody?" And I would have to say back to her, "Because I'm black and I'm a female." And like her saying that and embedding that in my head? *Ev-er-y day.* She would drop me off at school and be like, "*Why do you have to work harder than everybody?*" "*Cuz I'm black and I'm a female!*" That would be like what I would say back to her. And like just keeping that in mind? And always knowing that like: things were gonna come up, like, *being* the only black kid in school, being the only <u>fat kid</u> in school, being the only . . . kid with a single parent in school, being the only kid that lived in the *hood*, in my school. Like it just kinda gave me enough grit to be able to just be confident enough to *go* to Moun' Holyoke, ask for help when I need it, and just kind of like you know! Explore.

But I think you find a lot of resilient characters. I mean, not only the students but people that teach. And I felt like I actually made, to a certain point, where I could sit down and say, y'know, "It's not that hard." So I always felt like I could help them, because I understood.

Like, kids would be bipolar or manic. Okay, I—I can give you specific examples. I have one girl that ummm was given up by her mom—her mom already had mental health issues, and she was so mild and lovely. Y'know, she didn't look like everybody else did. She was, you know, the girls would call her ugly. "Oh, your butt too big, you nappy head, you too black." Y'know, whatever it is that they wanted to say about her. And she would take it and take it and take it. And one day she just . . . blew her top. Blew her top. She blew her top, and she fought a girl and ripped her hair out. Bloop! Got thrown in the ES [Emotional Support]. *Loved* her for it doing it, though. I'm like, "There you go, girl!" I mean, I don't—I don't condone fighting, but you know. She told me it, I read it in the thing, I was like, "Oh, God!" Sh—sh—she said she got tired of it. Tore the girl's hair out. She couldn't take it anymore!

I had another student that—he was a foster-care child. Oh, it's [a] horrible story. (*Very rapidly.*) His parents were addicted to drugs, he got *very* sick as a baby, they brought him to the hospital, they realized that he was being molested. So they immediately took him. Placed him into—I believe his father was molesting him. Put him into, y'know, a different foster home. And so he had, y'know, symptoms of being addicted to drugs as a baby *and* being molested, and— He would just have these fits of just— complete and utt— Docile any other time. *Complete* rage, like I'm talking about like ZZzerohh to a *million* in *one* second. Like—I have never seen an eleven-year-old pull—a—tree? Out—of— the—ground. OutTheGround! So angry that he pull—he could pull a tree out of the ground. So angry that he could take a table and turn it over. Beat somebody up.

I met him—how I met him was . . . This is a crazy story, it was my first—firsT . . . *week*. Working at Huey and, I *hear* somebody, just like blood-curdling scream. And I just see him running through the hall. Not—it's more—wasn't like a it was like a sssslow run, it was just like a very angry. He kinda Runs! Like! *This!* And he gets himself so worked up tha—he pours sweat, just like pouring down his body. And he's ripping things off the wall. "*Unhhh!*" Throwing stuff and throwing stuff and throwing stuff. And—I just *followed* him!

And we ended up down . . . stairs on the first floor. And all—I didn't know what to do. I had no idea, 'cause I'd never seen anybody do this before. Ididnotknowwhattodo. So all I did was grab him in the tightest hug. And just hold him, and hold him, and hold him, and hold him. And I just *held* him, 'cause I'm *really*, *really* strong. So I just held him and held him, like I put him in a hold? But it was like a hug. And I just *held* him until his body just collapsed. And he just started crying and crying and crying and crying on *me*. He was—I think at that point he was ten or eleven? It was like my third day working at Huey.

(*The musician leaves the stage.*)

NEVER GIVE UP

[Slide]

JAMES BALDWIN

FROM "A RAP ON RACE"—A CONVERSATION WITH DR. MARGARET MEAD
1971

"Walk on a Leaf"

"Walk on a Leaf"

(*This material comes from a seven-hour conversation that Mr. Baldwin had with Dr. Mead. It was both recorded and published as a book. Only Mr. Baldwin is performed for the purposes of this play. Musician is onstage and playing music as Baldwin speaks.*)

(*To the musician.*) If I may interrupt you for a moment. Luckily, I'm not fifteen, but if I were, how in the world would I find any respect for human life, or any sense of history? And history is a concept that exists in almost nobody's mind. (*To the musician.*) Go on, go on. According to the West, I have no history. I've had to wrest my identity out of the jaws of the West. What I'm trying to say is that if I were young, I would find myself with no models. And that's a very crucial situation. Because what we've done, the world we created. If I were fifteen, I would feel hopeless, too. So you see what we gotta try to, what we gotta try to face . . .

I read a little book called *The Way It Spozed to Be*. And it was poetry and things written by little black children, Mexican, Puerto Rican children. Land of the free, home of the brave. And the teacher had made a compilation of the poems these kids wrote. And he respected them. And he dealt with them as if they were—as a fact, all children are. As a fact, all human beings are . . . some kind of a miracle! And so something wonderful happened.

And so for me, that very tiny book, it's only thirty pages long, one boy wrote a poem. Sixteen years old, he was in prison. It ended, four lines I never will forget: "Walk on water / Walk on a leaf / Hardest of all / Is walk in grief."

So what I'm trying to get at, I hope, is that there is a tremendous national global moral waste. And the question is: How can it be arrested?

That's an enormous question. Look. You and I, we've become whatever we become. The curtain will come down eventually. But what should we do about the children? We are responsible, in so far as we're responsible for anything at all, we are responsible for the future of this world.

[Slide]

SHERRILYN IFILL

PRESIDENT AND DIRECTOR-COUNSEL
NAACP LEGAL DEFENSE AND EDUCATIONAL FUND
CONTINUATION OF AN ONSTAGE CONVERSATION BETWEEN
   MS. IFILL AND MS. SMITH
BALTIMORE, MARYLAND, JUNE 3, 2015

"So This Is It"

"So This Is It"

(*As in the prologue. Wearing a bright-colored jacket, onstage, comfortable living-room-type chair. Handheld microphone. Ms. Ifill is a public figure whose speech pattern and behavior is available to observe. Perhaps some indication that time has passed, less water in the pitcher, etc.*)

At one point, we had investments in our public school system. The end of serious investment in our public school system happened with the work of my predecessor, Thurgood Marshall, and desegregation. With *Brown v. Board of Education*. When you had massive resistance in the South. When the Prince Edward County school board decided to close the schools in Virginia for five years rather than—rather than integrate. Close the schools for *five years*. We—we broke our contract with education and we've never been able to get back to where we were. And so we've taken the mentality around those investments and we've placed them elsewhere.

So now, we're in a moment where people recognize? Across the board? That mass incarceration has gotten completely out of whack. And so this is a moment of reinvestment. And the question is: Where are we going to reinvest? And it's not just about dollars. But we have a mo— W-we're gonna do *something* with it. It's not gonna just go into the ether. It's gotta get invested somewhere.

And so while, yes, we want body-worn cameras, and we want things around policing, we also want a *massive* kind of investment of the kind that was the interstate highway system, you know? To focus on . . . how do we give people the opportunity to be people with a future. And education is a central piece of that. And so getting this understanding, what this moment means.

(*Pause.*)

There's a lot of heaviness and a lot of pain in—even in places that haven't had, you know, these incidents happen or had unrest happen in a very *public* way . . . There's a lot of heaviness. In this country, in this moment. There's a lot of pain.

We are—when I was a kid, I used to—my father was a—was a *huge* history *buff* and he was a *race* man, and so we watched, you know, every documentary that was *on* about the civil rights movement, and I remember feeling like I had *missed* it. "Darn it! It looked *great*, it looked *fantastic*, and I *missed* it!"

And so what I'd say to young people now is like: "So this is it!" You know, like, twenty years from now somebody will be saying, "I missed it!" Y'know?

And it's not just one, it's many. And *this* is the one. And as difficult as it is, and as heavy as it feels, there is a *privilege* in it. Because in this moment, this is the space where change can happen. It *only* can happen in a country as entrenched, particularly around issues of race, the moments when we move are the moments when we have to confront ourselves.

[Slide]

BRYAN STEVENSON

EXECUTIVE DIRECTOR, EQUAL JUSTICE INITIATIVE
FOUNDER, NATIONAL MEMORIAL FOR PEACE AND JUSTICE
MONTGOMERY, ALABAMA

"Injury"

"Injury"

(*A world-class orator whose speaking indicates a knowledge of classical rhetoric. Seated in a room at the Legacy Museum: From Enslavement to Mass Incarceration. A very simple gathering room with chairs and a podium. At the back of the room is a long wall, against which are many, many jars of soil, from sites where African Americans were lynched in the US. Stevenson is muscular—toned, buff, which his tight-fitting clothing reveals. Simple shirt and pants, colorful string bracelet. Many videos of his public speaking and interviews are available. He walks along the wall where the jars are and then sits in a folding chair. Soft-spoken, composed.*)

All of these jars represent communities where people were lynched. This is just the state of Alabama. Downstairs we have jars from all over the country. And some of these were what we call "public spectacle lynchings," where thousands of people came downtown and watched, uh, black men, women, and children being burned alive.

What we do is we collect all the available information about the lynching, um, and sometimes it's very precise: It's on the courthouse lawn, as Sherrilyn has in her book. Or it's in the public square. It's at this park, and—and you can, um, you can go to that park. Those places are still recognizable. Some of these lynchings are as recent as, you know, 1949, 1950. Um, other times, it's not precise. It's like, "They took him from the jail, and they took him down the road, and somewhere between mile marker eleven and mile marker twelve, he was hanged." Or "He was killed."

This is American history. I mean, I don't think what we're doing is African American history. When I talk about it, I like starting with what happened to Native people. Because I think we are a post-genocide society. I think what happened to Native people on this continent was genocide. We killed them by the millions; we slaughtered them. But we didn't call it genocide because we said, "Those Native people are different." And that's when this narrative of racial difference really began to take shape. And because we could say that Native people are savages, and we could create a rhetoric about their diminished humanity, we didn't feel bad, uh, to abuse them, to—to kill them, to force them off their lands. And that experience is what I think made American slavery particularly vicious. I think the great evil of American slavery wasn't involuntary servitude. It was not forced labor. It was this ideology of white supremacy, this idea that black people are not fully human. And that ideology was something that happened to white people just like it happened to black people. White people actually began to think that they are better than black people. And that has done something really corruptive. Those are white people in that picture standing around that—that—that, um, that platform [of a lynching]. White people were involved in each and every one of those incidents. It was white people. And there is a way in which you can see the tragedy of this history.

Uh, I've been around a lot of people who are in really desperate situations. I—I did have a case, um, not that long ago where we tried to get involved, we tried to stop an execution, and the man was scheduled to be executed in thirty days. And, um, I quickly learned that he suffered from intellectual disability. Our courts have banned the execution of people with intellectual disability. And so we went to the trial court and said, "You can't execute him. He's intellectually disabled." And the trial court said, "No, too late. Too late. You should have raised that years ago." And I went to the state court, and they said, "Too late." The appeals court said, "Too late." The federal court said, "Too late." Every court I went to said, "Too late." And we went to the US Supreme Court, and finally the United States Supreme Court accepted our motion, they reviewed it, and then about an hour before the scheduled execution, the clerk called me and said, "Yeah, the Supreme Court's going to deny your motion. You're too late." And I got on the phone with this man—and it is the hardest thing I have to do in my work—and I said, "I'm so sorry, but I can't stop this execution." And the man did the thing I fear the most in this work: he started to cry. And, um, within a few minutes he started to sob. And I mean I—it's literally fifty minutes before the execution, I'm holding the phone, and the man is just sobbing. And then he said, uh, "Please don't hang up. There's something important I have to say to you." And he tried to say something to me, but in addition to being intellectually disabled, he had another challenge: When he got nervous, when he got overwhelmed, he would begin to stutter. And he began trying to say something, but he couldn't get his words out. And I think that was the thing that I found just overwhelming, because he was trying so hard to get his words out, and he couldn't. And he kept trying, he kept trying, he kept—you know. And that's when tears were just running down my face. I was holding the phone.

And then when he said to me: "Mr. Stevenson, I want to thank you for representing me. I want to thank you for fighting for me." And then the last thing he said to me was, "Mr. Stevenson, I love you for trying to save my life." I—there was something about that. He hung up the phone. They pulled him away. They strapped him to a gurney. They executed him. I don't know, "I can't do this anymore. I just can't." There was just—I don't know—there was something about it that just shattered me.

And I was thinking about how broken he was, and I just couldn't understand: Why do we want to kill broken people? I—that's one of the things I don't understand. What is it about us that when we see brokenness, we get angry? We want to hurt it. We want to crush it. We want to kill it. And then I realized: All of my clients are broken people. I represent the broken. Everybody I represent has been broken by poverty or disability or addiction or dependency or racism. And then I realized that the system I work in is a broken system. People with power are unwilling to get close to people who are suffering. They're locked into these narratives of fear and anger. They've lost their hope. They won't do uncomfortable things or inconvenient things. And in that moment, I said, "I don't want to do this anymore." And I was sitting there awhile just thinking and something said, "You better think about why you do what you do if you're not gonna do it anymore." And it was in that moment that I all of the sudden realized why I do what I do. And it surprised me. And what I realized is that I don't do what I do because I've been trained as a lawyer. I don't do what I do because it's about human rights. I don't do what I do because if I don't do it, no one will. What I realized is that I do what I do because I'm broken, too. And that's the—the discovery?

I—I—I don't think brokenness is something that we necessarily wear? It's—it's much more, um—it's about a consciousness. And I don't think it's a bad thing. I actually think it's in brokenness that we understand our need for grace, our need for mercy. It's actually brokenness that helps us appreciate justice. It's in brokenness that we—we begin to crave redemption. That we understand the power of recovery. It's the broken among us that actually can teach us what it means to be human. Because if you don't understand the ways in which you can be broken by poverty or neglect or abuse or violence or suffering or bigotry, then you don't recognize the urgency in overcoming poverty and abuse and neglect and—and bigotry.

But I even feel broken by this history. (*Responding to a remark.*) Oh, yeah. When I was a little boy, they—you know—polio shots, you—they wanna give everybody a polio shot. My county, there were no, uh, doctors, so they made everybody go to a building which was kinda like a—it wasn't a health center, it was like a big building. And everybody had to get their polio shot. I was like five. Black people had to get in the back—go through the back door. So we line up out back. And it was a cold day. They gave all the needle shots to the white kids before they gave any shot to the black kids. By the time they got to the black kids—they had little sugar cubes they were giving the [white] kids—they ran out of sugar cubes. The nurses were tired. And they just had lost their capacity to be kind to these little children. And so they were grabbing these black kids and giving them these needles. And my sister was in front of me, and when they—she was next, she was so terrified, she looked to my mother, and she said, "Please, Mom. Please, please don't let them do this." And they grabbed my sister, and they pulled her aside, and took the needle, and they jabbed it into her arm.

And then they came for me. And I remember looking at my mom, and I was the same way. And they pulled me aside, and they were about to jab me. And then all of a sudden I heard all of this glass breaking. And my sweet, loving mother had gone over to a wall, picked up a table of beakers and glasses and was slamming them against the wall. And she was screaming: "This is not right. This is not right. Y'all should not have kept us out there all day. This is not right." And the doctor came running in and said, "Call the police." And the two black ministers came running over and said, "Please, doctor. Please, sir. Please don't call the police. We're sorry. We're gonna get her out of here." One of the ministers fell to his knees. Was like just begging: "Please, please. Please give the other kids their shot." I haven't thought about this in a while. Fell to his knees. And he persuaded them not to call the police, uh, to give the other black kids their shots.

And so I got my polio shot. They didn't arrest my mom, which I was happy about. But you can't have a memory like that without it creating a kind of injury. A kind of consciousness of wrong-fulness. A consciousness of hurt. That's what I mean when I say I'm broken, right? I have that in my head. And what it means is that there has to be recovery. I can't just absorb it. I gotta—gotta respond to it in some way.

(*Responding to a remark.*)

Yeah, it is the weight. And it shadows. And it burdens. And it—and it, um, and—and it creates a kind of, uh uh, anxiety that requires a response. And that's the thing about it. I just think a lot of us were taught that you just have to find a way to—to—to silently live with your brokenness, with this injury, with that memory. And I don't think that's the way forward. I'm looking for ways to—to not be silent.

A burst of noise, sirens, police, chaos, the actual scene after parishioners at Mother Emanuel AME Church, Charleston, South Carolina, were murdered by Dylann Roof while at a prayer meeting on June 17, 2015. Actual news of events immediately following massacre. A cacophony of various newscasters and speakers, perhaps President Obama. For example: "The shooter walked into the Emanuel AME Church and opened fire. We do know there are several victims, but it's unclear at this time how many and if there are any fatalities." "Dylann Roof would rant about the controversial killings of African Americans Trayvon Martin and Freddie Gray." "Critics say that the banner should be put away for good after the racist murders at Emanuel AME Church." The video shows protests to take down the Confederate flag from the capitol building. A crowd is chanting, "Take it down! Take it down!"

[Slide]

BREE NEWSOME

ARTIST AND ACTIVIST
CHARLESTON, SOUTH CAROLINA

"Not a Whim Thing to Do"

"Not a Whim Thing to Do"

(*Young African American woman, late twenties. Charismatic. Simply dressed. Perfect posture. Speaks in paragraphs rather than sentences, and quickly. Has studied how to stay on message. Lots of footage of her on talk shows, etc.*)

Because the first rule that was established was that a full human being was a landowning white male! Here! That's what made you a full human being, that's what made you worthy of having a vote. And everybody else is some lesser form of human, which is *why* it's okay to whip someone because they haven't picked enough cotton for you, which is why it's okay to pretty much do whatever you wanna *do*! Because other people are not . . . human beings. But what I saw—so—what I saw, I think beginning with Ferguson, but especially with the massacre at Mother Emanuel was . . . this recognition that like this level of violence can still be present when we stand up and try to fight for equality. You know what I mean? The sixties felt so much closer, I think.

Even—even before the massacre happened at Mother Emanuel, I had actually had a conversation like several months before with one of the folks in Tribe, Yin, who lived in South Carolina, actually. He lived in Rock Hill. And he had remarked that like his dream action was to take the Confederate flag down in South Carolina. He was like, "Oh, man, that's something that I've always wanted to do." And I *agreed* with him on that. You know, and I had already been arrested before, and I really was not planning to be like a chronic-arrestee-type protester, but I told him even then, I was like, "Yeah, that's something I would go back to jail for, like, if we could take the Confederate *flag* down. That's something that I would, you know, risk going back to jail for." (*Silent laugh.*)

So then after the massacre happened, when the—when the massacre happened and they wouldn't even lower the flag to half-staff, that was kind of the snapping point for me. Like, how could we possibly get this flag down? Because back in 2000, somebody had put a ladder up against the pole, climbed to the top, set it on fire, and so then South Carolina built this like four-foot fence around it. Like, it wasn't that *easy*. But Yin had a friend named Todd. And *Todd* had actually gone down. And looked at it. And he knew a Greenpeace activist in New York who had experience, you know. Scaling trees and all of these things and so, he was like, "You know, I really think"—he was looking at it and he said—"you know, I think that it's really just hooked on there. And that somebody could probably scale to the top and just unhook it."

And so then we kinda came together at a meeting. But it was essentially, um, the coming together of two activist groups. 'Bout ten to twelve folks. Basically a Black Lives Matter group. We refer to ourselves as the Tribe? You had Black Lives Matter, The Tribe, which was . . . *mostly* black activists. And then you had these, like, environmentalist/Occupy activists, who were mostly *white*.

(*Shaking her head.*) I mean, it took a lot of—lot—of—trust. You know, because, I mean, I walked into this room and it was like, half the people in the room were folks I had *never seen* before. In my life. And here we were talking about going down to take down the flag, I mean, you know, at that time, it was, there was so much national attention. You know, on it, so I mean, it was a dangerous thing to do. I think it speaks a lot to Yin's character, the fact that we were all able to trust each other. It's Yin's heart. He was fighting before it was cool. And he's just very—he's very *true*! When—when he *called* me and said, "You know, I—I know somebody who's really talking about taking the flag down, and we could really make this *happen*," I trusted him.

There was just the practical question of "Well, who can do each of the roles?" Um, a lot of folks just weren't in position to get arrested. Several people are teachers and they just couldn't—Yin's a teacher, he has children. I mean, Yin wanted to climb the pole, like that was his dream to do that. Um, but his wife just had a lot of concern. You know. About him doing that.

And so, you know, I think when we looked at who was able to be arrested? To risk getting arrested—and who was physically able to climb the pole, that really narrowed it down to about three or four people. And I was the only person of color. In that group? And when we, you know, were like really thinking about it, we felt that it would be most powerful to have a black woman be the one to scale the pole.

I have this memory of everybody staring at me? (*Laughing.*) Now, maybe that's not how it happened. I stepped into another room to pray. It was kinda like, yeah, okay, I will volunteer but I kinda wanna take a moment?

I prayed just for clarity and guidance. (*Slow, careful, sitting up even straighter.*) I mean, I really felt it on my heart, that I was supposed to do this; that God had called me to do this? I didn't want it to just be some whim. You know what I mean? It's not a whim thing to do. I had no experience climbing.

Well, I mean, here we were really talking about like some real physical danger. I'd been arrested before, and I was never afraid. There was never a concern of you know there being harm—a physical harm—in like the first arrest, but this was really a situation where I could potentially be putting myself at risk. (*Focused, no emotion, matter-of-fact.*) A vigilante coming by and shooting me while I was on the pole. I mean, we were really more concerned about that than what the police might do.

But on the day [when we were going to take] the flag down, they had a Klan rally scheduled. For later that morning, and so we, that's part of why [we planned our action for so early]. In the morning.

Just to reduce the—the chances of somebody coming by, you know, and possibly having a gun. And, you know, we just discussed what we would do in that situation, because obviously I would be, well, I wouldn't be able to do anything; I'd be in a very vulnerable position on the pole. (*Matter-of-fact.*) But we agreed that everybody else would scatter.

(*Direct, clear, focused, no emotion.*) I mean, I really had to make peace with that. I mean, I was it was very—I mean, it was a moment of radical faith on my part.

I just like made this, you know, commitment—and I can't say anything to, you know, my family. That's when it beca—that's when I started to feel the fear a little bit more of like what I was really about to do. And then I felt like tremendous fear.

I think I prayed . . . I mean that's some of the most intense praying I've ever done. (*Laughing.*)

That's where I think the idea and the cause becomes greater than the person? Because in a lot of ways, it was kind of like, even if I didn't make it down the—the statement would still . . . you know. Be made. (*Strong.*) And that was—that was the point that we wanted to—to make that . . . this is how—this is how serious it is.

You know, I got involved in this movement in 2013, and it was like, "*Yes*, we recognize that we are in this new civil rights movement. This is like the wake of the Trayvon Martin case. Y'know, the fir—the first action that I participated in, where I got arrested, we were doing a sit-in over the issue of voting rights. And I remember—I remember being arrested, and we are just like sitting there with our hands handcuffed behind our backs and—and it just hit me, I was like, "Wow. There was like a time when people did this and didn't know they were going to make it out alive." But there was still the sense of separation? From the sixties? I could still recognize there was a *definite difference* between the situation I was in at that time and, say, John Lewis with the Freedom Riders. You know what I mean, do you understand what I'm saying? [But now] the—the sixties felt so much *closer*, I think.

I thought about Martin Luther King. I thought about Malcolm X.

But then I really had to focus on learning how to climb the pole.

I had about a day and a half. A Greenpeace activist from New York came down and taught me and so we went out—Jimmy—James Tyson—he's the white man who was arrested *with* me. And so we were on James's farm, practicing—we practiced on a lamppost. And then finally we were able to find a school that had a flagpole.

We weren't even actually sure exactly how the flag was attached. I had in my backpack scissors and pliers just in case. They were calling for showers actually at one point. Showers and possibly lightning so that was the other factor we had to deal with. There were so many factors. Once I was actually *on* the pole, I was like right there at sunrise. I think I had so much adrenaline—I think I had so much adrenaline pumping? That—that I was all right.

The police arrived when I was about halfway up. It wasn't—it wasn't long after I got to like, my key point, because when we were practicing, we figured that I wanted to get eight feet up?

Before the cops showed, so that they wouldn't be able to snatch me down and ironically, the fence that South Carolina put up actually helped us. Because it made it harder for the cops to grab me.

In fact, there was a moment when a police supervisor directed the two officers who were standing at the bottom to tase me. And that would have electrocuted me because, you know, I was on the pole. And James grab[bed] the pole, he turned around to them and he said, "If you electrocute her, you'll have to electrocute me, too."

And I think that's when they again became aware that, you know, there are folks standing around with cameras, and, you know, smartphones, and all these things, and so then they, you know, backed off.

Actual cell phone video of Bree taking down the Confederate flag on June 27, 2015, is shown. The musician enters. He regards the video of Bree taking down the flag. A young woman in the crowd whom we cannot see yells up at Bree, "Take your time, Bree!" On the video, a police officer shouts to Bree, "Get down off the pole, ma'am. Ma'am!" Bree: "You come against me with hatred and oppression and violence. I come against you in the name of God. This flag comes down today! The Lord is my light and my salvation. Whom shall I fear? The Lord is the strength of my life." In the film, the group assembled below Bree claps and cheers. As the video ends, the musician begins to play a riff on "Amazing Grace."

CONGRESSMAN JOHN LEWIS

US REPRESENTATIVE (D-GEORGIA, 5TH DISTRICT)
WASHINGTON, DC

"Brother"

"Brother"

(In his office in DC. Congressman's office, with traditional furnishings. Shirt, tie, perhaps a jacket, shoes. A seasoned storyteller.)

On our way. On this trip that we been takin' for the past thirteen years. I been going back every year since 1965. Back to Selma. To commemorate the anniversary of Bloody Sunday, that took place on March 7, 1965. But we usually stop in Birmingham for a day. And then we go to Montgomery for a day. And then we go to Selma.

But on this trip, to Montgomery, we stopped at First Baptist Church, the church that was pastored by the Reverend Ralph Abernathy. It's the same church where I met the Dr. Martin Luther King and the Reverend Abernathy. In the spring of 1958.

Young police officer—the chief—the chief, came to the church to speak on behalf of the mayor that was not available. And he gave a very movin' speech to the audience. The church was *full*. Black. White. Latino. Asian American. Members of Congress. Staffers. Family members, children and grandchildren. And he said, "What happened in Montgomery fifty-two years ago durin' the Freedom Ride was not right," he said. "Fifty-two years ago was not right. The police department didn't show up. They allowed a angry mob to come and beat you," and he said, "Congressman! I'm sorry for what happened. I want to apologize. This is not the Montgomery that we want Montgomery to be. This is not the police department that I want to be the chief of. Before any officers are hired," he said, "they go through trainin'. They have to study the life of Rosa Parks. The life of Martin Luther King Jr. They have to visit the historic sites of the movement. They have to know what happened in Birmingham and what happened in Montgomery and what happened in Selma." He said, "I want you to forgive us." He said, "To show the respect that I have for you and for the movement I want to take off my badge and give it to you."

And the church was so quiet. No one sayin' a word. And I stood up to accept the badge. And I started cryin'. And everybody in the church started cryin'. There was not a dry eye in the church.

And I said, "Officer. Chief. I cannot accept your badge. I'm not worthy to accept your badge. Don't you need it?"

He said, "Congressman Lewis, I can get another one. I want you to have my badge."

And I took it. And I will hold on to it forever. But he hugged me. I hugged him. I cried some more. And you had Democrats and Republicans in the church. *Cryin'.* And his young deputy assistant. A young African American. Was sittin' down. He couldn't stand. He cried so much, like a baby, really.

It was the first time that a police chief in any city where I visited or where I got arrested durin' the sixties ever apologized, or where I was beaten. Or where I was beaten. It was a moment of grace. It was a moment of reconciliation. [The chief] was very young, he was not even born fifty-two years ago. So he was offerin' an apology and to be forgiven on behalf of his associates, his colleagues of the past. [It's a moment of grace.] It means that sufferin' and the pain that many of the people have suffered have been redeemed.

And then for the police officer, the chief, to come and apologize. To ask to be forgiven. It—it felt so good, and at the same time so freein' and liberatin'. To have this young man come up. He hugged me and held me. I felt like, you know, I'm not worthy. You know, I'm just one. But many people were beaten.

It is amazing grace. You know the line in there, "Saved a wretch like me"? In a sense, it's saying that we all have fallen short! 'Cause we all just tryin' to just make it! We all searching! As Dr. King said, we were out to redeem the soul of America. But we first have to redeem ourselves.

This message. This act of grace, of the badge says to me, "Hold on." And "Never give up. Never give in." "Never lose faith. Keep the faith."

Even in this day and age for a city like Montgomery. For this young man, somethin' moved him. And it takes what I call raw courage. To go with the spirit. To go with his heart. His soul. He's a very, he's really a very interestin' man. I been thinking about callin' him. "How ya doin'?"

The only time somethin' happened like this before was a member of the Klan from Rock Hill South Carolina that beat me and my seatmate. On May 9, 1961, durin' the Freedom Ride. He came here to this office in February '09. His son had been encouraging his father to seek out the people he had wronged.

And he came in the office and said, "Mr. Lewis, I'm one of the people that beat you on May 9, 1961. I want to apologize." He said, "Will you forgive me?"

I said, "I forgive you. I accept your apology."

His son started cryin'. He started cryin'. I started cryin'. He hugged me. I hugged him. His son hugged me. And since that time, I seen this guy four times since then.

He called me "brother." And I call him "brother."

(*As the lights fade to black, the musician reprises his riff of* "Amazing Grace.")

ABOUT THE MUSIC

Marcus Shelby
COMPOSER AND BASSIST FOR *NOTES FROM THE FIELD*

It has been a great honor creating and performing the musical score for Anna Deavere Smith's play *Notes from the Field*. Our process began about five years ago, when she and I first discussed how music could support the play with its many different voices, movements, transitions, and dramatic inflections. Anna and I come from the same musical tradition, firmly rooted in the black church experience, and this became our starting point. The musical devices that we borrowed from this shared history included the dynamic interaction of call-and-response, improvisation, and the blues. We wanted to employ the blues as a central language, one that springs from field hollers, blues shouts, blues cries, work songs, complaint calls, sorrow songs, prison songs, and griot storytelling.

When we first met in New York City to discuss *Notes from the Field*, Anna shared several interviews with me. She talked about her research into what was beginning to be called "the school-to-prison pipeline." This inspired me to do my own research, and I began a personal journey to learn more about mass incarceration and the "prison-industrial complex." One of the first things I discovered was that early blues forms championed by Bessie Smith and other black female blues singers spoke often of the prison experience. Blues was the primary musical vehicle for expressing the multiplicity of black experience at the turn of the twentieth century, and prisons, workhouses, and death row were frequent themes. For *Notes from the Field*, I wanted to borrow from the power of blues-based music to support the characters. I gave some of the characters themes that recurred later in the play where appropriate, as with the young Native American, Taos, whose story connects to so many other stories that show our schools struggling to deal with kids surrounded by trauma.

Although we performed *Notes from the Field* many times in different cities and for different types of audiences, and the play evolved in the process, the score stayed pretty much the same. In our first workshops we combined tenor saxophone with live bass. By the time we opened at Berkeley Repertory Theatre in Berkeley, California, in 2015 for the first theatrical run, we had changed it to solo bass, with the performer (myself) onstage for the entire length of the play. Anna and I looked for moments where music could build tension and release in the play and for moments where I could verbally communicate and respond as myself within the play.

These moments came without too much discussion, as we wanted the flow of rhythm and sound to be pure and unscripted. For me, it was a normal impulse, because I verbally communicate with the full spirit of call-and-response in my natural habitat as a musician. We also discovered where music was *not* serving the play and made changes accordingly. In the summer of 2016, we opened in Cambridge, Massachusetts, at the American Repertory Theater, and the musical score was reset to accommodate new characters and set changes (though the basic musical content remained the same). The changes made for the Cambridge run and, later, the New York City Second Stage Theater run gave the score more impact. We were able to pinpoint the most effective moments and characters that music would support. Furthermore, I was now present onstage only for certain characters, and my presence was integrated into the video, lighting, and panels that supported the play. These changes provided a rhythm and musical flow that was consistent with our initial goals of reflecting call-and-response, improvisation, and the sound and joie de vivre of black life.

The score is composed for solo acoustic bass and comprises single-line melodies, double- and triple-stops to create harmonic moods, and rearrangements of spirituals. The main goal was to find the right moods, using simple-but-blues-inflected shapes that at times were reprised and rearranged. Anna's theatrical voice reminds me of the great blues singers of the early twentieth century, singers like Bessie Smith, Ma Rainey, Clara Smith, Alberta Hunter, and Mamie Smith, all of whom had a resonant, pure tone quality that was articulate and soulful. The common quality in all great blues singers is their ability to hear and respond to the bass, which provides the root of the harmony and regulates the time like a heartbeat. Anna's voice is buoyant, and her timbre is full and distinct, especially when undergirded by the dark tone of a bass. This made it possible for us to interact both musically and vocally throughout the play. Working with her onstage, I could look for spaces to interpolate musically and create harmonic moods, much in the way I would accompany a vocalist.

One of the things I have cherished most in composing and performing the music for *Notes from the Field* was the extraordinary amount of freedom Anna gave me as an artist to respond to her work. For me, performing with Anna every night was like watching John Coltrane play his saxophone. She was that present, and it affected me greatly. So much of organizing music for the characters in the play was a process of trial and error through workshops, previews, and initial runs. By the time we got to Second Stage Theater, we had found the right balance of music, including themes that had become an essential part of the fabric of the play. I am very thankful to Anna Deavere Smith for the opportunity of a lifetime.

October 1, 2018

ACKNOWLEDGMENTS

There are so many people who were essential to the Anna Deavere Smith Pipeline Project, of which *Notes from the Field* is the key element. Without the original group of social justice philanthropists who, in 2011, introduced me intellectually to what is variously called the school-to-prison pipeline or the poverty-to-prison pipeline, I would never have gone on this journey. They are acknowledged below with all of the others who supported the project financially.

I am eternally grateful to all the artists who extended their time and creative power to the play, the film, and the project mission. Theater is not a lucrative profession. Nonprofit movie-making is not lucrative. Many of the artists who worked on the play and/or film have robust professional lives and could have used their time and ideas elsewhere.

As I attempt to acknowledge everyone who helped out, if I have failed to do so, I apologize deeply.

And I extend my profound gratitude to the more than two hundred and fifty people who spoke with me here in the US and in Finland. Thank you, thank you, thank you, from the bottom of my heart, for supporting our artistic endeavor and the children whose lives we seek to improve with this book.

For making this book possible: thank you to my wonderful literary agent Gloria Loomis and to steady assistant editor Catherine Tung.

To my editor, LuAnn Walther—for this and all the times you have put me in print—thank you for your editing, your patience, and your vote of confidence.

Stephanie Schneider, for your invaluable assistance as I worked to turn the language of performance into this book.

Chief judge of the Yurok Tribe, Abby Abinanti, a forever thank-you to you and your tribal community for providing a watershed moment in my ongoing search to understand American character.

Kimber Riddle, Michael Bentt, Ann Hould-Ward, Daniel Irving Rattner, Cheryl Hendrickson, Lisa Fischer, Amy Stoller, Michael Leon Thomas, Alisa Solomon, J. Stephen Sheppard, and Allen Bromberger for being deep in the trenches with me, whether on the road, in a dressing room, over a meal or a drink, on a phone call solving this or that problem, or alone together in a rehearsal hall, still laboring over lines to learn or performance challenges to overcome when everybody else had gone home.

Marcus Shelby for your music and for rich conversations from the very beginning of this project.

Gary Goetzman, film producer, for moving production forward even after the death of Jonathan Demme, who was originally slated to direct the film.

Ann Beeson for introducing me to the phenomenon of the school-to-prison pipeline.

Carole Rothman and Sara Garonzik for walking into that first big meeting with funders and for supporting the project as a play before there was one word imagined. To Darren Walker for hosting that meeting.

Blake Alcantara, David Lockard, Zoë Norman-Hunt, Elise Sokolow, my through-thick and through-thin team, for your artistic and logistical support. Remember the hilarity and the surprise discoveries more than the tough times.

Russlynn Ali, Kavitha Mediratta, Diana Cohn, Mary Lou Fulton, Jory Steele, Claude Steele, Sean Reardon, Julia Mendoza, Michael Margitich, Brian Berkopec, Ellen Poss, Erlin Ibrick, Robert Sherman, Dan Zingale, Linda Darling Hammond, Ann Dowley, and Linda Goldstein for initial and continued conversations grounded in the reality of the issues addressed.

At the American Repertory Theater at Harvard University: Diane Paulus, Diane Borger, Diane Quinn, and Ryan McKittrick. At Second Stage Theatre, New York City: Carole Rothman, Christopher Burney, and Casey Reitz. At Berkeley Repertory Theatre: Tony Taccone, Susie Medak and Sarah McArthur. At the Philadelphia Theatre Company: Sara Garonzik and Bridget Cook. At Baltimore Center Stage: Kwame Kwei-Armah and Stephen Richard. For the LIFT Festival production at the Royal Court Theatre, London: Vicky Featherstone, Beki Bateson, and David Binder.

Leonard Foglia, director, for creating one gorgeous off-Broadway production and one practical tour-ready production of *Notes from the Field* for the theater. You are a meticulous poet. I'm honored always to be in your company.

Kristi Zea, director, for taking the lead at the request of the late Jonathan Demme and directing the film version of *Notes from the Field* with such generosity, grace, humor, and creativity.

Theatrical designers: Howell Binkley, Jules Fisher and Peggy Eisenhauer, Riccardo Hernandez, Elaine McCarthy, Alexander V. Nichols, Leon Rothenberg, Dan Moses Schreier, Tania Ribalow, Anthony Dickey, Maria Verel, Michael Ramsaur.

At HBO: Richard Plepler, Casey Bloys, Len Amato, Tara Grace,

Maria Zuckerberg, Angela Tarantino, Nyle Washington, Dennis Williams, Lucinda Martinez.

Film designers: Declan Quinn, Doug Hsuzti, Paul Snyder, Mary Bailey.

Nori Chia, Steven Sharesian, Rocco Caruso, and everyone at The Playtone Company. Frank Garritano, Gillian Appleby, Emily Cohen, and everyone at Show Shop.

Michelle Bosch, Robin Abrams, Julie Baldauff, Maxwell Bowman, Taylor Brennan, Cynthia Cahill, Catherine Clark, Azriel Crews, Brendan Fay, Peter Gangi, Alexandra Dawn Hall, Callan Hughes, Cynthia Kennedy, Dawn Marcoccia, Kimiko Matsuda-Lawrence, Jordan Miller-Surratt, Riley Mulherkar, Joshua Reid, Jennifer Roberts, Christopher Vergara.

Nicholas Apps, Elizabeth Burke, Lesley Cannady, Ann Marie Lonsdale, Margaret Moll, Lisa Silverberg, Liz Ogilvie, Roy W. Backes.

My dear friends at Stanford University who hosted an invaluable residency at a critical moment in the project's development: Jane Shaw, Wiley Hausam, and Harry Elam. Thank you for sharing your intellect, your community, and your resources with me.

Thank you Drew Faust, then president of Harvard University, for encouraging the Harvard community to attend and support the pre–New York production of the play and for the conversations that followed.

A special thank-you to Tony Taccone, Susie Medak, Diane Paulus, and Diane Borger for jumping on board for my very ambitious audience-engagement experiment, the Second Act Project. It was unwieldy at times. It was disruptive, and disruption is costly in many ways. Thank you for all of the logistics and the reorganization of your space and resources needed to pull it off.

Thank you to everyone who worked with us as a facilitator during the Second Act Project. Your willingness to ride the ambition of our civic engagement experiment, your patience, and your bravery were key to furthering the conversation about the topics of this play with thousands of audience members who saw the show in Berkeley, Baltimore, Stanford, Philadelphia, and Cambridge.

Additional workshops and residencies:

> Yerba Buena Center for the Arts, Charles Ward and
>   Marc Bamuthi Joseph
> Bard College, Gideon Lester
> The American Academy in Rome

Directors of early workshop versions of *Notes from the Field*: Leah C. Gardiner, Jasson Minadakis

Thanks to the Pipeline Project field research team, which included Sabrina Aviles, Edgardo Cervano-Soto, Lee Green, Julian Hamer, Pendarvis Harshaw, Brooke Haycock, Kelly Hommon, Melissa Howden, Nick Leavens, Thaddeus Logan, Deirdre McAllister, and Lori Nesbitt.

A special thanks to the staff of the Jasper County Detention Center in South Carolina, who extended to our field research team the kind of hospitality we never would have expected in a correctional facility. I will never forget that lunch spread and the wisdom you shared with me. I now know that some who work in prisons really "walk" with those inside the walls, while others of us are so far away.

Lead support for the Anna Deavere Smith Pipeline Project is provided by the Ford Foundation.

Major support is provided by the Silicon Valley Community Foundation, Panta Rhea Foundation; the Andrew W. Mellon Foundation; the Atlantic Philanthropies, a limited life foundation; the California Endowment; NoVo Foundation; Poss Family Foundation; the Charles Evans Hughes Memorial Foundation; and Open Society Foundations.

Additional support is provided by Agnes Gund, Jordan Roth and Richie Jackson, Mr. and Mrs. Robert K. Steel, Suzanne Farver Advised Fund at Aspen Community Foundation, Miguel and Jacklyn Bezos, Jeremy Smith, Arison Arts Foundation, Susie Tompkins Buell Fund, Alexandra and Paul Herzan, George Lucas Family Foundation, Ellen and Bob Peck, David and Susan Rockefeller, Daryl Roth, Robert and Laura Sillerman, Sarah Peter, Michael Margitich, the John P. and Anne Welsh McNulty Foundation, Ann and Tom Friedman, Roger and Vicki Sant, Melva Bucksbaum and Raymond Learsy, Patricia Phelps de Cisneros, the Crown Family, Tom Freston, Cultures of Resistance Network Foundation, Robert J. Caruso and the Kantian Foundation, Louise Grunwald, the Mimi and Peter Haas Fund, Nancy and Morris W. Offit, the Ronald and Jo Carole Lauder Foundation, Peggy Dulany, Benjie Lasseau, the Modern Language Association of America, Marilyn Machlowitz, Jill Lafer, Laura Bachrach, Cindy Hunter, Aleim Johnson, Sharon Achinstein, and several anonymous donors.

The LIFT engagement was supported by Mid Atlantic Arts Foundation through USArtists International in partnership with the National Endowment for the Arts, the Andrew W. Mellon Foundation, and the Howard Gilman Foundation.

The Pipeline Project is a sponsored project of the New York Foundation for the Arts.

. . .

Thank you to New York University's Institute on the Arts and Civic Dialogue for its collaboration on the Second Act Project.

Thank you to New York University for its continued support of my work: the Office of the Provost, David McLaughlin, Katherine Fleming, Diane Yu, John Sexton, Andrew Hamilton, Allyson Green, and the Tisch School of the Arts.

ILLUSTRATIONS

In *Talk to Me*, Anna Deavere Smith applies her rare talent to the language of political power in America. Believing that character and language are inextricably bound, Smith sets out to discern the essence of America by listening to its people and trying to capture its politics. To that end she travels to some of America's most conspicuous places, like the presidential conventions of 1996, and to some of its darkest corners, like a women's prison in Maryland. Along the way she interviews everyone from janitors to murderers to Bill Clinton himself. Memoir, social commentary, meditation on language—this book is as vastly ambitious as it is